The
Hafod Landscape

An illustrated history and guide

by Jennifer Macve

Ymddiriedolaeth yr Hafod   2004   The Hafod Trust

The Hafod Trust gratefully acknowledges the financial support of Adfywio in the production of this book.

Picture Credits and Sources
The source and copyright owner of each picture is indicated alongside it (for cover and title page, see below). Those marked NLW are reproduced by permission of Llyfrgell Genedlaethol Cymru / The National Library of Wales. Other institutions that granted permission to use their images are Archaeoleg Cambria Archaeology, the National Museums & Galleries of Wales, the National Trust Photo Library, Derby Museums & Art Gallery, and the Forestry Commission (FC).

We are particularly grateful to Phil Smith for making available his excellent photographs. Thanks are due also to Prof. G.E. Bentley Jr., Christopher Gallagher, Christopher Gibbs, David James, the Piper Estate, Eric Thomas, Richard Broyd, Eilish Carr, Richard Crompton, Jennifer Macve, Donald Moore. The pictorial map was drawn by Eric Thomas.

The author wishes to acknowledge the assistance of the following in the preparation of the text and layout of the book:
Prof David Bateman, Richard Broyd, Prof Harold Carter, Richard Crompton, Philip Ellis, David Harris, Gweneira Raw-Rees, Arwel Thomas, Eglwys Newydd PCC;
and the documentary sources listed below:
Batey, Mavis, "The English Garden in Welsh", *Garden History*, xxii, 2, 1994; Borron, J.R.E., "The Waddinghams of Hafod", *Ceredigion*, xi, 4, 1992; British Geological Survey, 1:50,000 maps; Essick, R.N., *William Blake's Commercial Book Illustrations*, 1991; Fletcher, J., *Where Truth Abides: extracts from the diaries of the 4th Duke of Newcastle*, 2001; Hallett, R.A., A.P. Ledger and G.L. Pendred, "Scenes from Hafod on Derby Porcelain", *WHGT Newsletter* 6, 1992; John, Brian, *The Ice Age*, 1977; Jones, O.T., *Memoirs of the Geological Survey (Special Reports, Vol. XX)*,1922; Kerkham, Caroline, "Hafod: Paradise Lost", *Journal of Garden History*, xi, 4, 1991; Linnard, W., *Welsh Woods and Forests*, 2000 (2nd Ed.); Lloyd, Thomas, *The Lost Houses of Wales*, 1989 (2nd ed.); Macve, J. "A History of the Hafod Estate", *Gerddi*, ii, 1, 1998/9; Moore-Colyer, R.J., *Land of Pure Delight: Selections from the Letter of Thomas Johnes of Hafod, 1748-1816, 1992*; Phibbs, John, *Views at Hafod* (unpub.), 2001; Sclater, A., *Hafod Conservation Strategic Plan*, 1992; Suggett, R., *John Nash: Architect in Wales*, 1995; Whittle, E. (Ed.), *CADW's Register of Parks & Gardens of Historic Interest (Carms., Ceredigion, & Pembs.)*, 2002; Yerburgh, D.S., *An Attempt to Depict Hafod*, 2000.
A fuller bibliography and extracts from historical sources are to be found in *A Documented History of Hafod*, compiled by the Hafod Trust in 1998.

Designed by Argraff, Rhos y Corn, St David's Road, Aberystwyth, Ceredigion, SY23 1EU
Printed by D.W. Jones, Beverley Street, Port Talbot, SA13 1DY
Published by the Hafod Trust, Hafod Estate Office, Pontrhydygroes, Ystrad-Meurig, Ceredigion, SY25 6DX. © 2004

ISBN: 0 9527941 1 X

Front cover illustration: "Piran Cascade entire" (1810) aquatint by J.Stadler from a watercolour by John "Warwick" Smith. Llyfrgell Genedlaethol Cymru / The National Library of Wales

Back cover: the Cavern Cascade. Phil Smith

Title page: Ladies' Walk, 1788: an oblong comport from the Crown Derby Hafod Service. National Museums and Galleries of Wales

Contents

INTRODUCTION

A visit to Hafod is a unique experience. Once one of the best known and most visited places in Wales, by the middle of the twentieth century it had been largely forgotten by the outside world; its house, farms, and old woodlands gone and its hills densely planted with conifers in the spirit of the times.

Now Hafod has been brought back to life, and the romance of its landscape can be experienced once again.

Over the past two hundred years the Hafod estate has changed hands a dozen times, only once being passed from father to son. Although each successive owner has left a mark, however small, as an historic landscape Hafod is unusual in being associated almost entirely with one man: Thomas Johnes (1748-1816). His vision has survived through changes of fortune and fashion, and remains the inspiration for the work of the Hafod project today.

Photo: Phil Smith

The upper Gentleman's Walk on Allt Dihanog

4

THOMAS JOHNES

Thomas Johnes was descended on his father's side from a family of Welsh squires who, over the centuries, had acquired a number of small properties scattered across Carmarthenshire and south Cardiganshire. Hafod was the most northerly and remote estate, and probably the least valuable, consisting mainly of bleak hills, boggy hollows, steep slopes and narrow valleys.

Johnes's grandfather, also named Thomas, had occupied Penybont farm, near Tregaron, before inheriting two manor houses: Dolaucothi from his father and Llanfair Clydogau from a childless cousin. With the latter came Hafod, which had been the home of the cousin's first wife, Jane Herbert. In the next Johnes generation were two brothers, Thomas of Llanfair Clydogau and John of Dolaucothi. John married locally and had one son and four daughters, the eldest of whom was Jane. Thomas looked farther afield for his wife, making a very good marriage to Elizabeth Knight of Croft Castle in Herefordshire.

The Knights had made their fortune in the burgeoning iron industry of the West Midlands and border counties, and invested much of it in purchasing and improving country estates. Elizabeth's father, Richard Knight, had bought Croft Castle in 1746, from the Croft family – who had lived there since the 11th century but had recently fallen on hard times – while her cousin, Richard Payne Knight, built himself an entirely new and architecturally influential castle at nearby Downton-on-the-Rock in the 1770s. On his marriage to Elizabeth, Thomas Johnes of Llanfair moved to Croft and settled into a comfortable and prosperous life.

Thomas Johnes:
a marble bust by Sir Francis Chantrey
National Museums & Galleries of Wales

It was into this north Herefordshire world of new money and new ideas that Thomas Johnes of Hafod was born, in 1748. The eldest of four children, he was born at Dinham House, the Knights' town house in Ludlow, and attended schools in Shropshire before being sent to Eton. Later he progressed to the University of Edinburgh, where he mixed with innovative and radical people among both tutors and peers, and also had an opportunity to explore some of the wild scenery and great estates of the Scottish Highlands. His education was further advanced by a tour of Europe in the company of Robert Liston, a wise and cultured friend who would later become an accomplished diplomat and who corresponded with Johnes throughout his adult life.

Returning home to the Welsh border country, Johnes found that his parents had remodelled Croft in the latest Gothic taste and were preparing the ground for his future life as a member of the gentry: a Parliamentary seat (he represented successively three Welsh constituencies), a military commission, a suitable social circle and before long, no doubt, a good marriage. His father introduced him to his Welsh properties and responsibilities by taking him on occasional trips to the Principality. Evidently their visits to Cardiganshire included at least one call on their tenant at Hafod, John Paynter. Paynter, a mine manager, had a thoroughly bad reputation in the district, but his letters show that he was captivated by his surroundings at Hafod. The younger Thomas Johnes fell under the same enchantment and by 1771 he was telling Robert Liston that he had found "Paradise".

Photo: National Trust Photo Library/Rupert Truman

*Croft Castle,
Herefordshire: the east
front and church*

One can only guess at how and when, over the following decade, Johnes began to entertain detailed plans for a life at Hafod. In 1779 he married for the first time, to Maria Burgh of Park Lettice in Monmouthshire. It is clear that she quickly became acquainted with Hafod – she presented its church with a set of silver Communion plate - and it is possible that they considered living there, once Johnes had inherited his father's estates in 1780. Maria's poor health, however, was a discouraging factor, and in April 1782 she died. After a short-lived attempt at a career in the diplomatic service, in which he failed to take up a post in Madrid arranged for him by Robert Liston, Johnes returned to Wales. By the end of 1783 he had married his first cousin, Jane Johnes of Dolaucothi, and had taken up residence at Hafod. Those with a more conventional view of life, in particular his mother, were scandalised both by his hasty marriage to a close relative of no means,

and by his abandonment of Croft in favour of an impoverished estate in one of the remotest parts of Wales.

Photo: R. Crompton

*Memorial tablet to Thomas Johnes's parents and
maternal grandparents, in the church at Croft Castle*

THE JOHNES HOUSEHOLD
AT HAFOD

For a while, the marriage of Thomas and Jane was kept secret, but it could not remain so for long once a child had arrived. Their daughter, Maria Anne, was born in June 1784. She was always known by the romantic name, Mariamne, or within the family as Mary or Min. It has been suggested that a second child, a son, was born in 1786 and died in infancy. This is based upon a brief baptismal record in the church register: "on 9th August: Evan, son of Thomas Johnes." It seems unlikely, however, that this was a child of the Hafod family, for the following reasons: one would expect a lengthier entry for the squire's son; Evan was not a name ever used in the Johnes family; and there is no corresponding burial record. At that time surnames were a relative innovation in Wales (outside the squirarchy), and spellings were fluid, so Evan was more probably the son of a local farmer or miner named Jones. Twenty-five years later, a young man by the name of Evan Jones was to be found living in one of the Hafod lodges.

Mariamne remained an only child: doted upon, precociously intelligent, and deeply interested in the natural world. Tutors were brought in to help her acquire the usual accomplishments – music, drawing, languages – but she also became a talented botanist, from early childhood corresponding with Sir James Edward Smith, founding President of the Linnaean Society. At the age of ten, however, Mariamne developed an illness that was to prove chronic and very distressing. Theories as to its identity range from a genetic disorder through tuberculosis and rheumatic fever to congenital syphilis. She was afflicted with sudden fevers and rashes, tumours, weakening of the limbs and curvature of the spine. For a time she was unable to walk, and was fitted with a steel brace to support her and straighten her frame. Although by her late teens the worst seemed to be over, the illness probably had a lasting effect on her health and appearance. There are no portraits of her as an adult, apart from an informal sketch by George Cumberland, and no potential marriage partners were ever discussed. Her parents were cautious of taking her on long journeys and introducing her into society. In 1811, just after her twenty-seventh birthday, whilst in London, she died after a short bout of illness.

From f.47r of Cumberland's Sketchbook among the Cumberland papers of E.B. & G.E. Bentley, Jr.

The only known adult portrait of Mariamne Johnes, aged 18, with her Italian music master. An ink and wash sketch signed "GC" and inscribed "Miss Johnes and Sig. Viganoni 1804".

Hafod was very much the Johneses' main home, and they seldom went away for long, though Thomas had to visit London to attend Parliament. House guests were a regular feature, some of them staying for many weeks at a time. Jane's three sisters all made extended visits to Hafod, and one, Maria, who never married, became a long-term resident. She was almost certainly taken for granted by Jane (to whom she sometimes referred as "my Ladyship"), but was a loyal companion to Mariamne, helping to nurse her and staying with her in Bristol when she was receiving medical treatment there. Relations with Thomas's family were cool to say the least, but he was on good terms with his sister Charlotte and her husband, John Hanbury Williams, who liked to visit Hafod. Johnes's varied and sophisticated circle of friends were always welcome; two – Sir James Edward Smith and George Cumberland – both published books about Hafod, while Sir Uvedale Price was so captivated by the area that he built himself a picturesque, Nash-designed villa – Castle House - on the seafront at Aberystwyth. Scholars, poets, painters, and agriculturalists all made the arduous journey across the hills to enjoy hospitality at Hafod.

THE HOUSE

No pictures or descriptions of the old manor house at Hafod survive; its site probably lies close to or beneath the Johnes house. Originally it had been one of about thirty farmsteads within the Cistercian grange lands of Cwmystwyth, but after the Dissolution in 1539 it became the main residence of the Herbert family, formerly of nearby Dolgors. Thomas Johnes lived in it for a while during construction of its successor, which appears to have been an entirely new build.

The architect for the new Hafod was Thomas Baldwin of Bath, who was more usually known for designing neo-classical town buildings. At Hafod he created a house that was classical in its

Hafod House: watercolour of 1795 by John "Warwick" Smith, showing the house and early outbuildings as they were in 1792, before Nash's alterations

symmetry but Gothic in detail, with pointed windows, pinnacles, crenellations, and projecting corner pavilions. It was faced with Bath stone, which, being relatively prone to weathering, was not a particularly good choice for an exposed Welsh hillside. The main front, with entrance hall, music room and drawing room, faced south-west down the valley. The dining room, with bay window, and assorted smaller rooms looked out on to the east lawn. A detached service and stable block stood south of the house and can be seen on early pictures. Passing close to the house on its north side was the parish road from Pontrhydygroes to Cwmystwyth, roughly on the line of the present track from Lower Lodge to the church car park.

The new house was finished in 1788, but before long Johnes was planning improvements. He wanted more space and more privacy. In 1790 he obtained permission from the Court of Quarter Sessions to close the parish road and replace it with a new one farther north (part of the B 4574). To emphasise the new arrangements he built lodges across the old road – which had become the west and east drives – known as Lower Arch and Upper Arch. Both are now gone, though we have images of Lower Arch. He also built an entirely new drive, entering the estate at the present Upper Lodge (then called "Iron Gate") and taking a gentle downhill route for about a

mile, with glimpses through woodland to the river and Nant Peiran. "A sudden turn, most judiciously managed" brought the drive round the end of Middle Hill to approach the house from the south, necessitating the demolition of the stables. This would be the main approach to the house, bringing visitors from the inn at Devil's Bridge or direct from the turnpike road that crossed the bleak hills to the east and descended through Cwmystwyth.

In 1793 Johnes recruited a new architect, to alter the house itself. John Nash, then relatively unknown, was living in Carmarthen (having left London in haste and heavily in debt) and undertaking commissions for the public authorities and gentry of south-west Wales. At Hafod, Nash built a new range of domestic offices to the north, grouped around two courtyards, and at the north-east corner of the house an imposing octagon library, with a circular window at the top of its domed roof and an internal gallery. Opening from the library was a conservatory, running for 70 feet along the south-facing rear wall of the stables.

Nash may also have done other work around the estate, including the new lodges, glasshouses in the kitchen garden, the gateways with Coade stone decoration in the Flower Garden, and the first, cottage-style inn at Devil's Bridge. Relations with his client, however, became strained and they

Watercolour of Hafod House by Lord William Clinton, fourth son of the Duke of Newcastle. Drawn in about 1836, it shows Johnes's curving drive, the glazed colonnade and the Duke's alteration to the roof of the octagon library

Collection Christopher Gibbs

did not part on good terms. A few years later, Nash appears to have been the author of a proposed new design for Hafod's main front, portrayed in a striking watercolour by J.M.W. Turner, but Johnes did not take it up. In future Johnes would speak of Nash's contribution in a less than complimentary way: when, in 1807, the house was gutted by a devastating fire, he remarked to a friend, "all Nash's buildings are gone, & you will say, perhaps, no loss".

The loss by fire of the underinsured house, together with pictures, furniture, and irreplaceable items in the library, could have spelt the end for Hafod, but by careful budgeting and the sale of timber from Coed Hafod, Johnes found the means to rebuild. Baldwin was again brought in, to reconstruct the house within the surviving shell, though some alterations were made. There were no garrets, making the main rooms higher, and the octagon library was rebuilt without a gallery but with Anglesey marble columns supporting a dome with lantern light. As fire precautions, the

libraries had metal doors, heating was by Russian stoves, and the family bedrooms were on the ground floor. The colonnade on the south-east front became a second, "hardy" conservatory, glazed in winter; in the pavilion at its east end was Mariamne's study.

After Mariamne's death in 1811, her parents stayed on at Hafod until 1815, when they moved to Dawlish. Thomas Johnes died the following year and Jane in 1833. In the intervening years a lengthy wrangle over Hafod's legal title took place in the Court of Chancery. The house was not, as is often thought, left empty – a family named Churchill occupied it in the 1820s and had three children born there – but it was certainly neglected. When the 4th Duke of Newcastle took possession in 1833 he was obliged to do major repairs to the leaking roofs and weathered stonework. For the latter he seems to have used Portland stone, which is of a harder quality than Bath stone. The octagon library was remodelled in the fashionable oriental style, with an onion dome

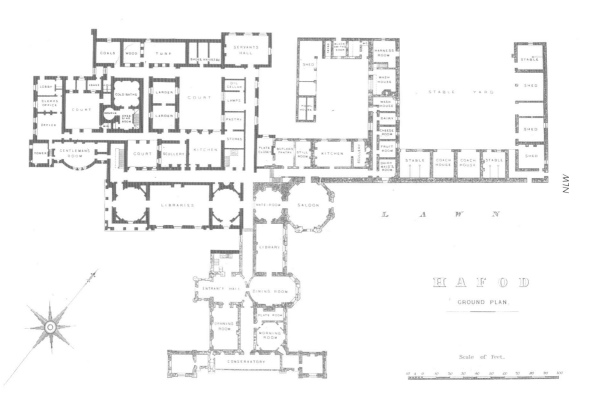

Ground plan of the mansion, prepared for a sale catalogue in 1870 but believed to be based on a plan by Anthony Salvin. The rooms with a darker outline are his additions of the late 1840s.

The mansion site and Coed Hafod from Middle Hill

surmounted by a glass spire, and alterations were made to the outbuildings and interior. The main conservatory was demolished.

A major phase of rebuilding began (but was never finished) with the purchase of Hafod in 1846 by Henry de Hoghton, owner of Hoghton Tower in Lancashire and heir to a baronetcy. The architect Anthony Salvin was employed to build a massive extension incorporating a grand enfilade of rooms, internal courtyards, new offices, and a tall bell tower. Designed in a heavy Venetian style and built of local stone, it sat oddly with Johnes's delicate Gothic house. By leaving it incomplete and with a duplication of rooms, Hoghton made the house unmanageably large and may have sown the seeds of its eventual destruction. Although John Waddingham, who bought Hafod in 1872, finished some of the bare rooms, demolished surplus offices, and built a new stable block, the maintenance of the house was an ever-expanding burden to subsequent owners.

By the mid-1940s the house was empty and dilapidated, and a brief hope that it might become an hotel came to nothing. In 1947 it was purchased by asset-strippers who held an auction, in 1949, at which all fixtures and fittings (including such essentials as floors and stairs) were sold off. They also blew up the clock tower. The forlorn shell, with surrounding land, was bought for the Forestry Commission in 1950. Unable to find anyone interested in rescuing the house, the

FC let a contract for the demolition of Hoghton's wing. In 1958, when further attempts to find a use for Johnes's house had led nowhere, it was demolished with explosives. The buildings and wall around the stable yard were retained, though a two-storey block on the west side was then knocked down in the 1970s. John Waddingham's stables continued in use for storage until 2001, when the Hafod Partnership obtained funds from the Heritage Lottery Fund to convert them into offices. One wing still contains its original Victorian stable fittings, and is currently occupied by logging horses.

The loss of the house at Hafod is much to be regretted. There have been many great houses lost in Wales, some much older or more architecturally distinguished than Hafod, but the house here was a focal point from which the walks radiated and which when first seen was "vastly striking and exhilarating", later to be enjoyed again when glimpsed unexpectedly from the walks through openings between the trees. But to temper this sense of deprivation, one should remember that a house can compete unfairly with a landscape for attention. Johnes himself became impatient with visitors who wished to spend their time trailing through his rooms and peering at his possessions:

Such is the curiosity of the world to see a House, when nine in ten neglect to go through the walks which are <u>worth</u> seeing.

11

HAFOD AND THE PICTURESQUE

Hafod is regarded by landscape historians as one of the finest examples of "the Picturesque". This term is used to define a particular set of aspirations and attitudes to landscape design, which were prevalent for a relatively short time but proved enormously influential in the long term. A glance at the type of scenes shown on modern greetings cards, for example, will demonstrate how the Picturesque has shaped our view of the "ideal" landscape.

By the middle of the 18th century, "picturesque" was already in use, as an adjective, to describe landscapes that had the qualities of a painting. Up to that time, painting landscapes for their own sake rather than as a backdrop to a military scene or portrait was little practised in Britain, so to gentlemen visiting Italy on the Grand Tour the landscape pictures of the Italian School came as a revelation. Returning to their country estates, pioneering landowners began to reshape their pleasure grounds in the manner of a peaceful and

A Hafod scene exhibiting essential elements of the Picturesque: broken ground, cascading water, mossy rocks, gnarled native trees.
Sketch by Thomas Jones of Pencerrig, 1786

evocative scene in the Roman campagna, as portrayed by such artists as Claude Lorraine or Gaspard Dughet. The fashion for an informal landscape, with lakes, clumps of trees, and classical buildings artfully arranged, soon spread among their peers and imitators, and a new profession, that of landscape gardener, came into being.

Against every fashion there is a reaction, and to some this visual style grew to seem too artificial and formulaic. Its premise of using an imported aesthetic to smooth over a rich and varied natural landscape was viewed as misguided, and its opponents sparked off a vigorous and sometimes spiteful debate that preoccupied artists, thinkers, landowners and gardeners to an extraordinary degree. This movement to create a more home-grown and natural landscape style was known as the Picturesque. Its adherents admired and celebrated the landscape of the upland areas of Britain, making sketching tours to seek out and define truly picturesque scenes, and attempting to design their own estates using the principles of intricacy, roughness, variety and surprise: creating an idealised "natural" appearance.

Thomas Johnes of Hafod was reaching maturity at a time when this shift in attitudes was taking place. His education and travels had not only exposed him to a great variety of landscape and artistic experiences but had also added an idealistic, social dimension to his outlook. And back home in Herefordshire he had the good fortune to be able to associate with the two great Picturesque theorists of the day: his friend and neighbour Sir Uvedale Price of Foxley, and his cousin Richard Payne Knight of Downton. Everything combined to produce an individual who would make Hafod a showpiece of the Picturesque and a place to challenge accepted ideas about managing an estate.

Unlike Knight and Price, Johnes published no weighty volumes outlining his philosophy of the Picturesque, nor did he leave any detailed record to show how he went about the task of designing his walks and the scenery through which they passed. There is nothing to suggest that he employed a professional landscaper, though he did acknowledge the strong influence of William Mason's lengthy poem *The English Garden* (2nd edition, 1783). Mason was a friend of the Rev.

Photo: Forest Life Picture Library

"Sublime" scenery in the Ystwyth Gorge

William Gilpin, an influential figure in the Picturesque, who, by publishing descriptions of his sketching tours around Britain in search of picturesque scenery, started a new genre of travel writing and set out precise guidance on how to identify, compose and if necessary embellish a suitable subject for drawing. Mason's poem applied similar principles on a much smaller scale; he promoted the concept of the picturesque circuit walk, by employing which a landowner could create the Gilpin effect within his owns grounds. A winding path would take the visitor to a series of carefully composed but seemingly natural scenes, using landforms and plantings to shape or "hide and reveal" the view.

At Hafod Johnes was very fortunate in owning a landscape that already contained the essential components of the Picturesque: steep topography, rocks and crags, old woodland, rushing streams and cascades. To this, guided by Mason, Johnes applied "the well directed efforts of the hand of art", according to one visitor (Thomas Rees). Another writer, B.H. Malkin, made a slightly different assessment, remarking that "in laying out the

grounds, art has been no further consulted, than to render nature accessible". In saying this, Malkin intended a compliment, for part of the code of the Picturesque was that all should appear natural, with walks and bridges flowing organically through the landscape, and nothing contrived or forced. In fact, Johnes blasted rocks, moved earth, and diverted streams, but it was so skilfully done as to prevent the observer from detecting any artificiality.

It would be misleading, however, to portray Johnes's Hafod as a series of carefully designed walks through an untouched Welsh wilderness. Certainly in the Ystwyth Gorge and on parts of the Gentleman's Walk there are scenes of nature untamed that merit the 18th century term "sublime" – that is, giving rise to feelings of terror, awe and astonishment. There were further sublime experiences to be had in the Devil's Bridge area of the estate. But variety and contrast are central tenets of the Picturesque, and the wilder parts of the estate were incidents in an essentially domesticated landscape. While walking through the dense woods of the upper Gentleman's Walk, one was occasionally offered a reassuring view down onto meadows and fields, to the Flower Garden, the church, or the house.

Conversely, the view from the main windows of the house was of a grand assemblage of woodland and cascades across the river with bare hilltops of rough pasture above. The landscape was a patchwork of different types of land-use, with the fields of the home farm intermingling with woods and new plantations, and the visitor was led through a succession of views where the scale, content, and emotions evoked were continually varied.

GEOLOGY AND NATURAL HISTORY

Hafod lies just to the east of a major structural feature: the Teifi anticline, an eroded upward fold that runs NNE to SSW and brings to the surface the oldest rocks in Ceredigion, from the early Silurian and late Ordovician systems. Crossing this line from west to east is another important feature, the Ystwyth Fault, a tear in the earth's crust that caused massive movements of the ground, both vertically and laterally, and can be traced for some twenty-five miles. In places the Ystwyth river exactly follows this line of weakness, for example in the two-mile stretch from the Flower Garden to the bridge at Pont-rhyd-y-groes, but elsewhere the two diverge, and the river has cut itself a narrow gorge through harder rock, as at Dologau and Maenarthur.

Older than the Ystwyth Fault and in places disrupted by it are other faults, running SW-NE and containing mineral lodes. Sometimes they are detectable as depressions in the ground; for example, one such fault, that runs beneath the mansion site, creates gaps in the two ridges to the east, at Hawthorn Cottage and Hafod church. Others cross the southern hills and can be seen in stream beds as exposures of white quartz. Scattered around the estate are a few shafts and levels from short-lived mining schemes or explorations but, fortunately for the survival of the landscape, the lead and zinc deposits in these Hafod lodes were generally of poor quality and did not attract mining activity on a large scale.

Photo: Forest Life Picture Library

A river pothole carved into resistant gritstone beds in the Ystwyth Gorge

The Silurian strata underlying Hafod, deposited some 350 million years ago as sediments in a marine basin on the margin of a continental shelf, consist of grits, sandstones, shales, and mudstones. Within that broad description they vary considerably in age, composition, and hardness, and they are deformed by dense folds and faults so that, where they appear as outcrops, they will be seen to be inclined at different angles and directions of dip. The rocks found north of the river, and in the south-eastern Hafod hills, all fall within a classification known as the Devil's Bridge formation, but the seemingly uniform face of Allt Dihanog, traversed by the Gentleman's Walk, is composed of different, somewhat older strata, associated with the Teifi anticline to the west and appearing on the surface as a succession of narrow, north-south bands. One minor formation exposed here in just a few restricted locations has been named by geologists the Hafod Member, and is characteristically thinly bedded, shelly, and containing phosphatic pebbles.

The effects of glaciation are evident at Hafod. The Ystwyth valley was deepened both by ice and by massive flows of meltwater: water-worn rock faces can be found high above the present river level, and tributary streams were left in hanging valleys from which they now descend to the river in fast-flowing torrents with frequent cascades and falls. Rocky summits standing above the ice were accentuated while lower hilltops were smoothed. In shallow valleys and basins, such as the mansion fields and Pendre Meadow, are thick deposits of till (boulder clay), formed within and beneath moving ice sheets and typically occurring as a stony, orange-coloured clay that clings stickily to boots. On the margins of the river are found patches of coarser material, the sands and gravels deposited by glacial outwash. These would once have been more extensive, clogging the valley and shaping the course of the river: a build-up of gravels at what is now Dologau fields may have diverted the Ystwyth from an earlier course and contributed to the creation of the gorge.

The bottom of the Hafod valley lies at about 550 ft (170m) above sea level, rising to 800 ft (240m) at the church and Tŷ Coch, and the estate enjoys a climate that is noticeably wetter and cooler than the coastal plateau to the west. It is occasionally swept by severe, damaging storms, and periods of

Golden Spindles (Clavulinopsis fusiformis), a woodland fungus common at Hafod

Photo: David James

prolonged rain cause local flooding and landslips. Its general moistness is, however, a great advantage, when combined with its pollution-free air, in supporting a rich flora, particularly among lower plants. Lichens, mosses, liverworts, and ferns thrive in its patches of old woodland and damp, sheltered combes, and the whole site is particularly rich in fungi, with the unimproved pasture around the mansion site supporting a community of waxcaps of international importance. Certain species of lichen and fungus occur nowhere else in Wales. Among the larger flora of interest, both in their own right and as encouragers of biodiversity, are some fine old parkland and forest trees, including a few surviving from Johnes's time. The largest beech trees are thought to have been planted by Johnes, and include specimens that appear to have been

A massive, multi-stemmed beech

Photo: Christopher Gallagher

bundle-planted: that is, two, three or more young plants placed in the same planting hole so that they grow together in picturesque forms. Most of the oaks to be found at Hafod are sessile, but a few stands of pedunculate oak have also been identified. There are also some mature small-leaved limes and wild cherries, but sadly no large sweet chestnuts are still standing, though evidence from stumps shows that they were once a feature of the mansion fields and Cae Gwartheg. The Cedar of Lebanon on Middle Hill is known to have been planted by Johnes, but the two Wellingtonias date from the mid-nineteenth century.

More than half of the Hafod estate lies within the Elenydd Site of Special Scientific Interest. This was originally designated primarily as a means of protecting the Red Kite, for which the Hafod hills and valley were a last stronghold when the population was at its most threatened. Today kites are a common sight over a much wider area in mid-Wales and numbers are in the low hundreds, but Hafod remains one of their most favoured breeding areas. Other raptors, including buzzards, goshawks, and sparrowhawks are to be seen, and the numbers and variety of species of smaller birds are increasing as conifer plantations are thinned or removed. A second SSSI – that of the Gro Ystwyth Shingle Heath – falls partly within Hafod; it consists of six scattered pieces of riverside shingle which are unique in their geomorphology and ecology due to their glacial origins and mineral content.

Hafod has its share of invasive species, with *Rhododendron ponticum* being a particularly resilient and widespread weed. While it is futile to attempt to eliminate it entirely, it is hoped that a programme of removal combined with the expansion of grazed areas may bring it under control. Along the river's edge and some of the drives, patches of Japanese knotweed pose a problem and are regularly treated. Self-seeded alien conifers spring up in open spaces after felling of the parent crop. The grey squirrel is the most prevalent animal pest, doing widespread damage to trees, especially vulnerable saplings. That other bane of forests, the deer, is absent apart from very occasional sightings of lone individuals.

THE HISTORY OF HAFOD

EARLY HISTORY

Lying on the edge of the Cambrian Mountains, the Hafod valley is an area that has always been one of the remotest and least productive parts of Wales, sparsely inhabited and lacking good communications with the outside world.

For periods earlier than the Bronze Age, there is an almost total absence of evidence for human activity in the mid-Wales uplands. Although not plentiful, there are monuments from the Bronze Age (c.2500BC-c.600BC), including round barrows and standing stones, as well as mining artefacts found at Copa Hill above Cwmystwyth, all suggesting a settled population. At this date the hills around the Ystwyth valley are believed to have been well wooded, and human settlements may have been located in the intervening valleys, but unequivocal evidence for them is lacking. In the fields surrounding the former mansion at Hafod there is a small number of circular depressions, and it has been suggested that these are prehistoric house platforms; though other, more recent, origins are also possible.

Although succeeding centuries, including the Roman occupation, left little or no physical trace in the landscape of Hafod and its surroundings, it is generally accepted that the Ystwyth valley was settled and farmed long before the emergence of written records. It is probable, given the frequency of hafod and hendre place-names, that the population practised transhumance, with farming families living in their lowland farm or "hendre" during the winter months but migrating with their flocks to the hill pastures for the summer and occupying their "hafod" or summer house. The traditional types of landholding, however, were in places subsumed into a new structure imposed by religious houses, and Hafod Uchdryd (to give its full name, the second part being a personal name) was one such place, with its origin as an estate arising from the creation of an administrative unit within a monastic economy.

Five miles south of Hafod lay the Cistercian abbey of Strata Florida (Ystrad Fflur), founded in 1164, which derived much of its wealth from agriculture, in particular sheep farming. Its extensive land holdings were organised into large farms known as granges, of which one, the Cwmystwyth grange, covered territory that would later form the core of the Hafod estate. With the Peiran Mill (1km east of Hafod mansion) lying roughly at its geographical centre, the grange was subdivided into many smaller farms, each of which probably consisted of a farmstead encircled by small, cultivated enclosures which in turn were surrounded by rough pasture with open sheepwalk on the highest hills. The abbey made efficient use of other natural resources, having fish traps on the Ystwyth and also exploiting the lead deposits at

Old oak coppice growing on a rocky outcrop, drawn in 1786 by Thomas Jones

Cwmystwyth, where they may have had a smelting operation. It is often alleged that the presence of mines was to blame for the treeless aspect of the uplands in north Cardiganshire. However, clearance of woodland long pre-dated the appearance of large-scale mining operations, and was more likely to be the result of the deliberate creation of sheepwalks. At the same time, woodland itself was a valuable resource, and its survival on steeper slopes in sheltered valleys, such as Hafod, should be attributed to sensible management rather than historical accident. Regular coppicing and lopping provided a continual supply of leaf fodder and firewood, as well as the raw material for fencing and hurdles, tools, furniture, and charcoal. Early maps of Hafod farms show that each possessed a reserve of woodland, amounting to between 5% and 11% of the farm's total area.

When, in the 1530s, Strata Florida abbey was dissolved and its lands confiscated, the Cwmystwyth grange came into the possession of the Earl of Essex. A rent roll of ca.1540 shows that the grange then consisted of some thirty tenements let to an assortment of tenants; among the properties listed are Upper and Lower Hafod Uchdryd and several others which would later become estate farms. A century later, the former grange land was sold to John Vaughan of Trawsgoed (Crosswood), who almost immediately sold a large part of it to Morgan Herbert, the occupant of Hafod and nearby Dolgors. The Herberts established themselves as the squires of this small, remote estate, almost certainly financing their lifestyle from mining interests. Nothing is recorded of their development of Hafod other than the building of the first church (Eglwys Newydd) in 1620, but it seems reasonable to assume that their house was surrounded by pleasure grounds and that the woodland was well managed, perhaps with some new ornamental plantings. After five generations of Herberts at Hafod, the last remaining heir was Jane, who married into the Johnes family. Her father's will survives and stipulates that if she and her husband should die childless (as they did), his property should revert to his sister's family, but for whatever reason this wish was not carried out and Hafod stayed in the possession of the Johneses.

THOMAS JOHNES'S LANDSCAPE

The Hafod estate inherited by Johnes in 1780 was an awkwardly shaped holding of about 7,000 acres, with inliers of property belonging to other owners. It included two large farms adjacent to the demesne - Pwllpeiran to the north of the river and Bwlchgwallter to the south; also the Herberts' original home, Dolgors farm, to the north-west, three remote sheep farms in the hills to the east, and a detached fragment at Ffair-rhos, four miles south. Much of the land was unenclosed and treeless, ranging in quality from good hill pasture to bleak peat bog. However, the valley slopes near Hafod were well wooded, as the Jones sketches show (see below), with mossy, ivy-covered oaks, old coppices, large mature trees, and straight-stemmed, young standard trees. Here, in the core of what would become Johnes's designed landscape, there were important differences between the north and south sides of the Ystwyth, evident in early drawings.

On the north bank, the relief was very varied and the landscape domesticated, with large expanses of grassland. Two ridges, Middle Hill and Cefn Creigiau, projected towards the river and were covered with wood and pasture. Around them were meadows that may have been used as parkland for as much as two centuries; there were no obvious traces of medieval field systems and no old field names survived. On its northern edge the demesne was bounded by a steep wooded slope, Coed Hafod, curving in the west to pass closer to the river from which it was separated by long, narrow meadows. The parish road from Pontrhydygroes to Cwmystwyth ran at the foot of this slope, through the centre of the demesne, to join the turnpike to Rhayader (created 1770) a mile east of the church. The main buildings in this area were Hafod house, the church, and the old mill on the Peiran, though the last did not belong to Hafod when Johnes inherited (he acquired it from Lord Lisburne in 1790). Drives, tracks and paths must have connected these buildings with each other and with surrounding farms, and there may also have been some ornamental walks around the grounds. There is no record of any minor buildings pre-dating the arrival of Johnes, though some of the features shown in images

River above the First [Alpine] Bridge: aquatint by J.Stadler after John "Warwick" Smith (1810). The Lady's Walk can been seen on the left, with Middle Hill above it and Cefn Creigiau in the centre distance.

NLW

from the early period of his occupancy - a turret on Middle Hill, the "Alpine" bridge across the Ystwyth, and a cottage at Pendre – were possibly all inherited from the Herberts.

To the south, the dominant topographical feature was Allt Dihanog, a steep, north-facing slope along the river. The 1832 Sale Catalogue describes it as "part of Bwlchgwallter Farm": in other words, historically it had always fallen within that tenanted farm's land and the distinction continued to be made long after Johnes had taken it in hand. The whole slope was wooded, with the exception of a small, clear enclosure called Cae Gwartheg, which had a slightly gentler gradient and more open aspect, making it suitable for improved pasture or cultivation. Bwlchgwallter, south of the crest of the slope, had long been a Hafod farm and would have been connected to the house by a path or track, which may have crossed the river by a footbridge and/or ford in the vicinity of the present Alpine Bridge. At its eastern end the slope retreated from the river and here were located several smallholdings and farms - Penpompren, Tyloge,

Nant y Cae - which Johnes acquired and incorporated into his estate. Paths would have linked these cottages, and one track crossed the river by Pompren Mawr. This bridge, the predecessor to Dologau bridge and perhaps originally built by the monks of Strata Florida, was still in existence in 1781; after crossing it the track climbed north to pass close to the Peiran mill and then on to join the parish road. It is unlikely that there were any pre-Johnes "pleasure" paths on the south side of the Ystwyth, and this would seem to be confirmed by George Cumberland's remark that the "principal part of the artificial improved paths" were to be found here. The implication is that, on the north side, Johnes had been able to create a circuit walk by linking up and remodelling existing paths.

During his first ten years at Hafod, Thomas Johnes rationalized the estate into a more coherent shape by exchange and purchase of land, and increased its size to nearly 13,000 acres. Much of it was tenanted but, in the early years at least, Johnes had nearly 5,000 acres in hand, and here he was able to pursue three interrelated interests: forestry,

Sketch by Thomas Jones of the "Menagerie" pond, Pendre meadow, Cefn Creigiau and the distant woods on Allt Dihanog (1786)

farming, and landscape design. As regards the last of these, he had achieved great changes within the first four or five years, though tantalizingly little can be gleaned from documentary sources about his methods and intentions. In the autumn of 1786, the artist Thomas Jones of Pencerrig visited Hafod and recorded the landscape in a series of pencil sketches, some very detailed. Jones's accuracy and draughtsmanship are such that nearly all of his views are identifiable in the modern landscape, and it is evident that the two main circuit walks were already in place or well advanced. There are no sketches of the house – still under construction at that time – and very few of other buildings, though there is one of a

dilapidated thatched cottage, two of the Alpine Bridge, and two in which a turret can be seen on the point of Middle Hill. The last is mentioned by a visitor in 1799 but, oddly, by no other source. Some of Jones's views, along with other early pictures of Hafod, were used as the basis for illustrations on pieces of Crown Derby porcelain that made up the "Hafod service", produced in 1788. From these pieces we know that the Cold Bath was already in existence - the two images on porcelain being the only representations of it that survive - and that a cottage (the forerunner of Hawthorn Cottage) stood beside the pond at Pendre and was known as the Menagerie. Two ponds, specifically fishponds, are mentioned in

Derby Museums & Art Gallery

The Ystwyth near the Flower Garden, portrayed on a cream-bowl stand from the Derby Hafod Service (1788)

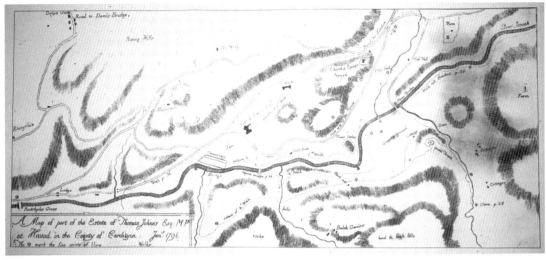

William Blake's engraved map of Hafod

early letters written by Jane Johnes, from which source we know also that kitchen garden and flower garden had been created by 1788.

A second important reference point comes with the publication, in 1796, of George Cumberland's modestly titled book, *An Attempt to Describe Hafod.* Cumberland (1754-1848), an artist, writer, and collector, had been introduced to Johnes by Richard Payne Knight, and no doubt surprised and delighted Johnes by revealing that he was already acquainted with the wild country around Hafod and the Devil's Bridge, having visited it on an adventurous walking tour in 1784. After their meeting Johnes wrote to him, in July 1794, urging him to visit Hafod and saying

I am anxious to shew you, who have seen this place in its original wildness, that by beautifying it I have neither shorn or tormented it.

Cumberland duly visited that autumn, spent two weeks exploring the estate and then returned to London to write up his experiences. His book is the earliest detailed account of the landscape, and is

Tyloge [Dologau] Bridge: aquatint by Stadler after J. Smith (1810). The view is taken from the south bank, looking downstream.

20

Entrance to Mariamne Johnes's Garden

Photo: J. Macve

invaluable for several reasons: it contains an enormous amount of information about the walks, the views from them and the type of land-use around them; it is written by someone who was highly aware of current ideas about the Picturesque and viewed the landscape in that context; and it contains the only map of Hafod produced during Johnes's time. Quite how this map was made is uncertain, but it is usually attributed to William Blake - a close friend of Cumberland – and certainly the lettering has characteristics of Blake's style. At the time Blake was helping Cumberland to master the techniques of engraving, so they may have worked on it together. The scale and proportions are far more accurate than one would expect from a simple sketch map, and it must be assumed that Johnes supplied a tracing of an estate plan to use as a base, but sadly no original plans survive.

By the time of Cumberland's visit Johnes had acquired some farms on the east banks of Nant Peiran and Nant Gau, north and south of the river respectively, from Lord Lisburne of Crosswood (Trawsgoed), and also two smallholdings, Penpompren and Dologau (historically always spelt "Tyloge"). This opened up new possibilities for extended walks and link paths, and Cumberland describes an unfinished walk being laid out along the south side of the Ystwyth gorge and continuing as far as Pentre Mill (in Cwmystwyth, which at that time was known as Pentre Briwnant). A new, stone-arched bridge, which would become an important practical and visual focal point in the enlarged demesne, was built at Dologau. The new layout of drives had also been completed by this time, and at Pendre, just east of the mansion, Johnes had established his home farm, where new buildings made to his own design were arranged in a crescent shape. Nearly all of the structures built by Johnes – cottages, lodges, bridges, cattle houses – were designed to complement the landscape but principally served a practical purpose. Unlike the great landscape gardens of preceding decades, Hafod had no temples, sculptures or grand follies. There were a few minor buildings of a mainly ornamental nature, including the Cold Bath and some covered seats and summerhouses, but these acted as incidents along the walks and made no bold statements of their own. As Cumberland and many later writers make clear, it was the walks themselves and the varied scenery revealed from them that were the glory of Hafod.

Cumberland remained one of Johnes's most regular correspondents and made further visits to Hafod, but unfortunately never realised his stated intention of publishing a second edition of his book. There are, however, many other works, including unpublished diaries, sketches and letters, from which one can build up a picture of developments at Hafod in succeeding years. *A Tour to Hafod*, by another regular visitor, Sir James Edward Smith, was not published until 1810, but describes the landscape in the 1790s and includes eight important coloured prints (plus another nine of the Rheidol valley). Based on sketches and watercolours done by John "Warwick" Smith, these show "set piece" views of the house, the river, and the most dramatic waterfalls. Reference is made in the book to the garden of Mariamne Johnes, though, in the early years at least, this was a private domain shown only to favoured guests. Designed in 1795 by James Anderson, a Scottish agriculturalist who had been advising Johnes on farming matters, it occupied what was probably an old quarry on the south-facing cliff edge at Pencreigiau. It provided a site for Mariamne to grow unusual plants, including alpines, and was laid out with paths, rock-cut steps, a moss-house, and an ornamental funerary urn, complete with inscribed sentimental verse, for a tame robin.

Johnes was a restless individual, continually looking for new outlets for his creative energy and imagination, and throughout his time at Hafod he made further additions to the designed landscape. In the late 1790s he built a "return walk" from the Cavern Cascade on the east bank of Nant Gau, and perhaps at around the same time replaced the

NLW

The double-arched bridge of Pont Newydd carrying the east drive above the upper Peiran Falls. Watercolour sketch by J. Parker, ca.1831.

"rude" Alpine Bridge by a two-arched wooden structure. Picturesque cottages for the gardener and bailiff were erected at Pen-creigiau and Pendre Uchaf, and in 1801-2 he demolished the old church (of which we have no visual record), to make way for a new church designed by the fashionable architect James Wyatt (see p.51). In 1805 he built new walks leading up to Mariamne's Garden and, on a rocky platform just below it, installed an obelisk, to commemorate Francis, 5th Duke of Bedford, who had died in 1802. Also in 1805 he constructed the chain bridge across the Ystwyth gorge, finally completing the New Walk that Cumberland had explored in 1794. His activities were disrupted by the loss of the house in the fire of 1807, and little was done in the next three years while the family lived at Castle Hill, Llanilar, and rebuilding work dragged interminably on. In 1809 it was announced that the Jubilee of George III (acceded 1760) would – in view of his poor health - be held a year early, as he entered the fiftieth year of his reign, and in honour of this

occasion Johnes revived an idea he had first had in 1806, for an ornamental stone arch crossing the turnpike road at its highest point, between Hafod and Devil's Bridge. The Arch was built that autumn and still stands. The last major addition to the landscape came in 1813-14, with the construction of a "new & most beautiful approach": the east drive, entering the estate at a new lodge in Cwmystwyth and crossing Nant Peiran by means of a bridge of two stone arches, one above the other, in an apparent imitation of the Devil's Bridge. Over the years Johnes also erased features from the landscape: a number of buildings shown on Cumberland's map, including the old mill and several farmsteads and cottages, simply vanished from the scene over the next few years. As well as documented alterations to the landscape, there are many that can only be discovered from field evidence; these include viewing platforms and spur paths, significant plantings, and manipulation of streams to create water features.

FARMING AND FORESTRY

In Johnes's time, as now, Hafod was a working landscape, and all his visitors alluded to his experimental and innovative work in tree-planting and farming. Of the two activities, he regarded planting as the more important and his commitment to it was unwavering, in spite of a high rate of losses caused by climatic conditions, depredations by sheep, and poor quality plants. Johnes holds a place of honour in the history of forestry for his attempts to convert large areas of low-grade hill pasture into productive plantations. At the time there was considerable concern in Britain about the country's depleted woodlands, particularly with regard to timber reserves for ship-building (as compared with the enemy, France), and Johnes was rewarded for his efforts with Gold Medals from the Royal Society of Arts (RSA), prizes from the Cardiganshire Agricultural Society, and the sobriquet "the patriotic Mr Johnes" from visitors. His records of trees planted before 1807 were destroyed in the mansion fire of that year and later ones have not survived, so evidence is rather imprecise and anecdotal. Johnes's annual returns to the RSA give species and numbers of trees planted, as well as details of the type of ground chosen and fencing methods employed, but no locations are named nor any indication given as to whether old woods were being restocked or virgin sites planted. The numbers are impressive, and suggest that Johnes may have planted between three and four million trees in total, but this should be placed in perspective against high failure rates and a dense planting regime of 4,000 trees to the acre.

As a result of the above circumstances, two misconceptions have arisen. The first is that Hafod was devoid of woodland when Johnes acquired it, whereas, as we have seen, the demesne was well wooded. The second is that he covered thousands of acres of former sheepwalk with flourishing plantations; but the area described in a sale catalogue of 1832 as "plantation" amounts to only 473 acres, and a surveyor noted that the trees were far from flourishing. It still represents, however, an impressive achievement in an era when few landowners were attempting new planting on such a large scale and on marginal land. The new plantations were established on the higher slopes to the north and east of Hafod, with the most extensive areas lying on both sides of the turnpike road to Devil's Bridge. For the most part they were of European larch, a tree of a rather more picturesque appearance than the Japanese or Hybrid larches favoured by modern foresters. The 1832 catalogue lists a further 331 acres of woodland and 103 acres of wood with pasture, where much of Johnes's broad-leaved plantings must have taken place, in the form of under-planting or restocking. He is known to have planted oak, beech, alder, elm, birch, ash, and mountain ash, with further plantings of larch and Norway spruce in a few areas within the heart of the demesne. Today the evidence available from documents and field surveys is being used to replicate as far as possible Johnes's planting schemes in the designed landscape.

Johnes's farming activities were subject to alternating bouts of enthusiasm and disappointment. In such a remote location, a mixed home farm was important to ensure a reliable supply of essential produce, but in common with many of his class and generation Johnes went further, using his farm to try out new ideas and to instruct others. His crop rotation schemes, methods, and building designs were set out in his own book, *A Cardiganshire Landlord's Advice to his Tenants* (published in English and Welsh, 1800). Until 1806 his home farm, with its farmstead at Pendre, covered the fields and wood-pasture of the demesne and probably most of the land formerly pertaining to Pwllpeiran, Cefn yr Esgair, Gwaryrallt

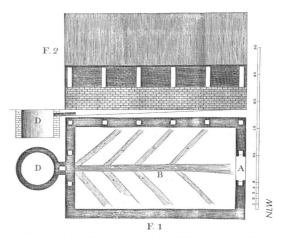

Plan and elevation of a covered, self-draining dunghill, as recommended by Thomas Johnes in "A Cardiganshire Landlord's Advice to his Tenants".

and Tyn y Clyttie farms. One visitor stated that Johnes owned 200 cattle and between 2,000 and 3,000 sheep of assorted breeds. Exotic (for Cardiganshire) breeds of both cattle and sheep were introduced, and equally exotic cheeses made. To secure a year-round supply of fresh meat Johnes attempted to grow enough hay to keep cattle through the winter, and was said to have so improved the meadows in the demesne (including the mansion lawns) that eighty cows could be supported where before there was fodder for only two. He used a system of dams and channels to direct stream water on to the meadows, in order to enrich them with "fructifying particles". Arable fields were also to be found in the demesne and beyond, growing staples such as potatoes, oats, barley and turnips, and more experimental crops, including wheat - of which Johnes was especially proud, having been assured by his neighbours that it would not succeed at such altitudes.

By 1806 Johnes had decided that he could no longer justify the high capital input and poor returns of the Pendre home farm. He demolished the buildings, taking care to recycle the materials, and let out most of the land to tenants, keeping in hand only the meadows and wood pasture of the demesne, lying between the river and the parish road to the north. He then turned his attention to developing the New Farm, with a purpose-built farmstead, known as Gelmast, located about 1km north of Pwllpeiran, and 2,000 acres of land reaching from there far into the hills to the east. Johnes's intention was to improve poor hill-grazing land and peat bog by draining, paring and burning, and laying down new grass, and then to use the new grassland for sheep. This was in spite of setbacks he had experienced in earlier years with breeding and raising sheep, under a regime of his own devising. By 1812, however, he had once again become disillusioned and had disposed of his sheep flock, largely because of the difficulty of preventing their invasion and destruction of his plantations. In the meantime he had found a new enthusiasm, for Fiorin grass *(Agrostis stolonifera)*, by which he hoped to develop good upland pasture for cattle. This, together with further tree-planting and improvements at Devil's Bridge, occupied much of his time in his last three years at Hafod, when he and Jane persevered with their life there, despite being left as "miserable branchless trunks".

THE PICTURESQUE TOURIST

To Johnes, improving his estate was an eminently worthwhile aim in itself and one which would bring economic benefits to the surrounding country, as other landowners (he hoped) followed his lead and farm productivity and employment increased. At the same time, though, he wished to set the seal on his achievements by ensuring that Hafod would be visited, admired, and commented upon by people of influence and discernment. South and North Wales had for some years been attracting growing numbers of travellers in search of the Picturesque, but Cardiganshire, with just a few small towns of little consequence and nowhere for people of quality to stay, was lagging behind. Writers such as Thomas Pennant, William Wyndham, and William Gilpin, who became celebrated for their Welsh tours, all failed, in their first editions at least, to describe the country around Devil's Bridge. Gilpin's influential *Observations on the River Wye, and Several Parts of South Wales …* was first published in 1782, but by 1787 a second edition was in prospect. Hearing of this, Johnes visited Gilpin and showed him drawings of Hafod by Thomas Jones, urging him to include a description of the estate in the new edition. Gilpin duly obliged, providing a glowing write-up of the Lady's and Gentleman's Walks and mention of a longer "riding", in the edition published in 1789. At about the same time, Aberystwyth was becoming known as a watering-place, and so the number of travellers venturing into the area began to show a steady increase.

Following the lead set by owners of some English estates (Studley Royal in Yorkshire, Hawkstone in Shropshire), Johnes determined to provide purpose-built accommodation for visitors, thus enabling them to stay several days and explore the area in depth. In 1790 he acquired a farm adjacent to the Devil's Bridge, where the wild and sublime scenery provided an exciting complement to Hafod. Here he selected a spectacular site for a "little public cottage", close to the junction of two turnpike roads but otherwise completely remote and at a judicious distance from his own house. In 1795 it was enlarged into an inn, the Hafod Arms. The publication in the following year of *An Attempt to Describe Hafod* did much to persuade tourists to include Hafod and the Devil's Bridge in their

The first Hafod Arms and the Rheidol gorge, in a sketch of about 1800, possibly by the Rev. John Breedon

itinerary, and when some of these visitors then published their own accounts of the landscape, Hafod's fame spread, with each successive summer seeing greater numbers arriving. The first Hafod Arms underwent at least one further extension before Johnes decided, in 1814, to erect a new building, larger and more formal in appearance, which survives as the main building of the present hotel (though the attic floor and dormers are a later addition). At the same date the upper bridge – the middle layer of the three today - was partly rebuilt, and Johnes was responsible for the design and manufacture of its ornamental iron railings, which are still in place.

In the early years, visitors typically were young men, travelling light on foot or horseback, and arriving at the inn singly or in twos or threes – people such as Cambridge undergraduates Samuel Taylor Coleridge and Joseph Hucks (1794), or the clergyman and antiquarian Richard Warner (1797 and 1798). They would bring with them a diary and usually a sketchbook, in which to record their enthusiastic response to the sublime and picturesque wonders all around. On the whole their needs were simple, and they were appreciative of the good food produced on the inn's own farm and the wine supplied from Hafod's cellar. As Hafod's renown grew, however, the Hafod Arms saw more family parties arriving by post-chaise and even the occasional earl in a grand carriage. With them they brought servants and sometimes a hired artist. Increasingly there were also day-trippers from Aberystwyth, some of whom showed more interest in consuming Johnes's fine wines than in exploring his landscape. In later years one finds Johnes remarking sadly on the arrogant attitude of some visitors who, he felt, abused the hospitality and innocence of local people. He seemed to become aware of the contradiction inherent in tourism to wild and unspoilt places: by their very presence his visitors had changed his Paradise for ever.

HAFOD AFTER JOHNES

After Johnes's death in 1816, the sale of Hafod was held up for many years by legal wrangles arising out of two circumstances. Firstly, a sale initiated in 1814 to an industrialist, Thomas Claughton, became stalled (Claughton was something of a serial defaulter, having also reneged on an agreement to buy Lord Byron's Newstead Abbey). And secondly there was the complex problem of Johnes's "encroachments": areas of Crown common land, over which he had rights but not legal title had been annexed to the estate and in some cases enclosed and planted. Once these matters had been resolved by the Court of Chancery, the estate was put up for auction in 1832.

The purchaser was Henry Pelham, 4th Duke of Newcastle (1785-1851), who in August 1834 paid £62,038.16s.8d for Hafod. It is often alleged that the Duke bought Hafod as a retreat, to escape the many enemies he had made through his vigorous opposition to Parliamentary reform, but the evidence does not support this. He retained his main residence at Clumber, Nottinghamshire, and a house in London, using Hafod rather as a holiday home. He would visit for several weeks in the late summer and autumn, usually accompanied by some of his adult children, and would enjoy shooting, making excursions, visiting Aberystwyth for the theatre and sea-bathing, and riding around the estate making plans for improvements. At first he was full of ambitious schemes, including a proposed new village, and he spent generously on a major renovation of the mansion, enlarging the Hafod Arms at Devil's Bridge, converting the Cwmystwyth lodge into a school, and repairing or replacing estate buildings, both those in hand and those on tenanted farms. But by 1841 he was experiencing financial problems and became acutely aware that Hafod brought in insufficient income to pay for its day-to-day running. By 1843 he was looking for a purchaser.

We know that under the Duke the estate was managed in a conventional manner, with none of the experimentation and risky capital ventures that characterised the Johnes years. He had a mixed home farm, based at Pwllpeiran, and spent considerable sums on draining the fields, excess water being an ever-recurring problem at Hafod. The woods were well managed, with regular sales of poles, posts, and firewood, and a saw pit, workshops and sheds were constructed at Pendre yard in 1837. It is unlikely, though, that the Duke created new plantations other than some small areas at Allt y Dafarn and Devil's Bridge. Planting and other landscape changes may have been made, or at least planned, in the environs of the house, perhaps by William Sawrey Gilpin (who had worked for the Duke at Clumber) but as yet the details are unclear. The grounds at Hafod continued to be open to visitors, but the fashion for taking tours to wild places in pursuit of the Picturesque had waned and few descriptions of

Photo: Donald Moore

LEFT: The Duke's Drive crossing the west lawn

RIGHT: An extract from the Hafod sale catalogue of 1855 (NLW)

HAFOD: Waymarked Walks and Historical Features

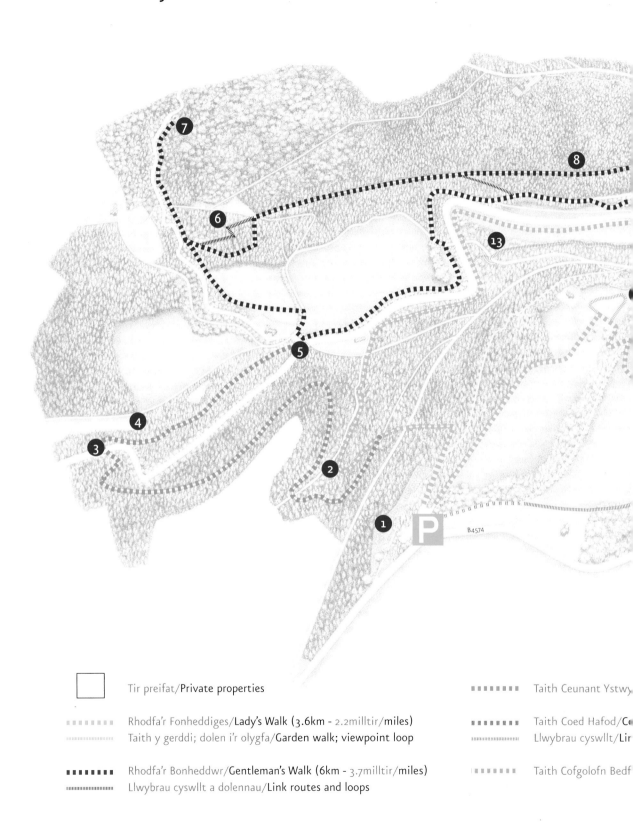

Tir preifat/**Private properties**

.... Rhodfa'r Fonheddiges/**Lady's Walk (3.6km - 2.2milltir/miles)**
mmmmm Taith y gerddi; dolen i'r olygfa/**Garden walk; viewpoint loop**

■■■■■■■■ Rhodfa'r Bonheddwr/**Gentleman's Walk (6km - 3.7milltir/miles)**
mmmmm Llwybrau cyswllt a dolennau/**Link routes and loops**

.... Taith Ceunant Ystwy

.... Taith Coed Hafod/**C**
mmmmm Llwybrau cyswllt/**Lir**

.... Taith Cofgolofn Bedf

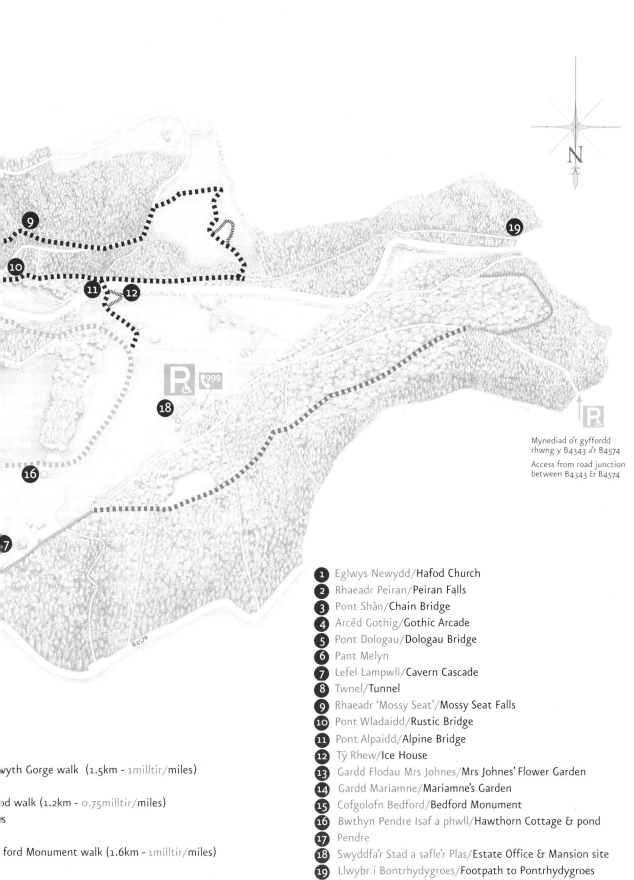

N

Mynediad o'r gyffordd
rhwng y B4343 a'r B4574
Access from road junction
between B4343 & B4574

1 Eglwys Newydd/**Hafod Church**
2 Rhaeadr Peiran/**Peiran Falls**
3 Pont Shân/**Chain Bridge**
4 Arcêd Gothig/**Gothic Arcade**
5 Pont Dologau/**Dologau Bridge**
6 Pant Melyn
7 Lefel Lampwll/**Cavern Cascade**
8 Twnel/**Tunnel**
9 Rhaeadr 'Mossy Seat'/**Mossy Seat Falls**
10 Pont Wladaidd/**Rustic Bridge**
11 Pont Alpaidd/**Alpine Bridge**
12 Tŷ Rhew/**Ice House**
13 Gardd Flodau Mrs Johnes/**Mrs Johnes' Flower Garden**
14 Gardd Mariamne/**Mariamne's Garden**
15 Cofgolofn Bedford/**Bedford Monument**
16 Bwthyn Pendre Isaf a phwll/**Hawthorn Cottage & pond**
17 Pendre
18 Swyddfa'r Stad a safle'r Plas/**Estate Office & Mansion site**
19 Llwybr i Bontrhydygroes/**Footpath to Pontrhydygroes**

wyth Gorge walk (1.5km - 1milltir/miles)

od walk (1.2km - 0.75milltir/miles)

s

ford Monument walk (1.6km - 1milltir/miles)

B4574

HAFOD,

IN SOUTH WALES.

THE FAME OF HAFOD is so far and wide-spread that any attempt to pourtray its *sublime and surprising beauties* is as unnecessary as it would be vain and ineffectual.

No spot in Europe, perhaps, possesses such an astonishing and wonderful combination of Scenery; Scenes blending such romantic and enchanting BEAUTY with objects of such awe-inspiring grandeur!

IT IS ONE OF NATURE'S WILDEST AND MOST FAVOURED HAUNTS.

It has been described by MEYRICK, CUMBERLAND, MALKIN, HUTTON, and others, but no force of language can convey a full or just idea of its

GREAT AND VARIED NATURAL BEAUTIES,

WITH ITS

Superadded Embellishments of Art, Genius, Taste, and Wealth.

MAJESTIC MOUNTAINS AND ROMANTIC ROCKY PRECIPICES,

CLOTHED WITH

FORESTS OF OAK AND LARCH,

OPENING TO RECEIVE

" The torrent's awful roar beneath,"

AND RIVERS FOAMING IN CATARACTS, POOLS, AND CAVERNS,

Or winding in more peaceful and expansive streams through lovely Glades and cultivated Grounds, are among its most striking Features ; these, with

DELIGHTFUL DRIVES AND WALKS OF ALMOST BOUNDLESS EXTENT AND NEVER-FADING BEAUTY,

THROUGH ITS VAST AND FINELY CONTRASTED

WOODLANDS AND PLANTATIONS,

Form the magnificent Home Demesne, surrounding *the elegant and princely Mansion,* and embracing the beautiful Church and various ornamental Buildings appertaining to this noble Domain.

THE WONDERFUL DEVIL'S BRIDGE,

IS AT ONE EXTREMITY OF THE PROPERTY, AND

THE GRAND AND TREMENDOUS FALLS,

AT THAT CELEBRATED AND INTERESTING SPOT, WITH

THE HAFOD ARMS HOTEL,

(Entirely rebuilt in 1839,) form a portion of the Estate.

The SITUATION OF HAFOD is secluded, but the old turnpike-road passes through the Estate, about 16 miles from RHAYADER, 16 from LLANIDLOES, and 14 from ABERYSTWYTH, the latter favourite and fashionable town giving it the advantage of SUPERIOR SEA BATHING.

It is now by railroad only about 14 hours' journey from London, which will be diminished by more than one-half on the completion of the intended railroads, some of which are already in progress. The Estate lies in the direct line of the proposed Manchester and Milford Haven Railway.

The most *direct* route from London at present is by railway to Shrewsbury, thence posting through Welshpool and Llanidloes to the Devil's Bridge, where the Northward side of this vast Domain commences, amidst the most wild and highly picturesque Mountain and River Scenery skirting a portion of the fine turnpike-road, which, passing through the property (partly distinguished by its Larch Plantations), reaches the Mansion from the Bridge in about 4 miles, or by coach from Shrewsbury to Aberystwyth, and thence to the Devil's Bridge, distant 12 miles.

From the North, Hafod may be reached by rail through Chester to Oswestry, whence a coach runs to Welshpool and Aberystwyth, or Hafod may be reached by posting from Welshpool as above.

Arrangements have been completed that, early in June, several additional coaches will run from Shrewsbury *via* Welshpool, and the opening of the Great Western Line to Hereford will also greatly facilitate the means of transit to Hafod.

the estate survive from this time. There is nothing to suggest that the Duke made any significant alterations to the walks and views in the demesne, other than one brief reference to improvements being made around the Peiran Falls in 1843. Contemporary sketches show that Johnes's two-arched bridge here had been replaced with a straight span, and a footbridge crossed the stream below the falls at the Rustic Alcove. From the Duke's time come the earliest references to the icehouse and to a vinery in the kitchen garden, but both may have been built by Johnes. A new cottage for the gardener was constructed or at least begun within the kitchen garden. Two landscape changes still bear the Duke's name: the "Duke's Drive" was built in 1837, crossing the lower lawn and acting as a by-pass to the house, and in the following year the "Duke's Pond" was created in an upland hollow 1km north of the mansion, but whether its purpose was primarily recreational or practical (i.e. for water supply) is not explained.

In 1846, having finally paid the settlement for the Crown lands and seen off a railway scheme that threatened Hafod, the Duke succeeded in selling the estate. The buyer, Sir Henry de Hoghton, is mainly remembered for his major alterations to the house (see p.11), but his other activities on the estate are poorly documented. The setting of the house was remodelled, perhaps to a design by W.A. Nesfield or his son A.M. Nesfield, who were related by marriage to the architect Anthony Salvin. Johnes's informal sweep of lawns was interrupted by a ha-ha, terrace, and flowerbeds. Hoghton was probably also responsible for re-routing the approach to the house from the south; where Johnes's drive had rounded a "careless and elegant bend" followed by a gentle dip and then ascent to the front door, there was now a dramatic rock cutting, framing the widened façade of the house, and a straight drive on a raised causeway. Hoghton created at least one new plantation: at Cae Gwartheg, the field in the south-west corner of the demesne, which had been arable land on the Tithe Survey compiled at the beginning of his tenure.

Both Newcastle and Hoghton had purchased farms adjacent to Hafod, and its size had reached nearly 14,000 acres by 1855 when it was sold at auction. The new owner was William Chambers (1809-1882), a prominent liberal and industrialist from Llanelli. Having the misfortune to have been born illegitimate, he was unable to inherit his father's properties in South Wales and Kent, and therefore bought Hafod as a country residence where he could raise his large family and, he hoped, derive an income from the estate's natural resources. Chambers was a member of the Scottish Arboricultural Society and his returns to that body show that he found an abundance of

The stables, built by John Waddingham in 1882 and now housing the estate office.

young and mature timber at Hafod, from 20 to 70 years old, including "700 acres of larch" (probably an exaggeration). A water-powered sawmill was built beside Nant Peiran, and over a 12-year period Chambers felled, processed and sold both soft and hardwoods. From an examination of an estate plan of 1864 it would appear that for the most part plantations were thinned rather than clear-felled, and that at least one new area of plantation (on Cefn Dyrys) was created. At around this time lead-mining in North Cardiganshire was at its peak of activity, providing a ready market for timber and also affecting the Hafod landscape directly to a small extent, with Chambers granting leases to mining companies on outlying parts of the estate and engaging in some exploration himself within the demesne.

Severe financial difficulties obliged Chambers to put Hafod up for auction in 1864, but only some outlying parts were sold, including the inn, farm, and embryonic village at Devil's Bridge. Another auction was planned in 1870 but did not take place. Eventually, in 1872, Hafod was sold to John Waddingham of Guiting Grange, near Cheltenham, and a long period of stability and wise investment began. In addition to reorganising the house and building a new stable block (dated 1882) and nearby barn, Waddingham made changes to the curtilage, including a conifer avenue planted along the front drive and a terrace wall built to the south and west of the house. Improvements were made to many estate farms and cottages, a new west lodge built, new buildings erected in the kitchen garden and the gardener's cottage enlarged. Waddingham was an energetic forester, favouring European larch, and parts of the demesne were cleared, fenced and re-planted during his time. The Devil's Bridge portion of the estate, sold by Chambers, was bought back.

After John Waddingham's death in 1890, Hafod passed to his younger son, T. James Waddingham. He and his wife took a particular interest in church matters and under their direction Eglwys Newydd was restored, a mission church built at Devil's Bridge, and both Hafod and Devil's Bridge provided with a vicarage. It is believed that the grounds and gardens were well maintained during this period but no detailed records survive. A small area behind the mansion was planted with shrubs and possibly ornamented with built features, and became known as the Japanese Garden. In the early part of the twentieth century the estate derived a steady income from the sale of timber and wood products, and T.J. Waddingham was active in encouraging the Vale of Rheidol Railway scheme (opened 1903) which reduced transport costs.

However, with no direct heir and in the knowledge (confirmed on his sister's death in 1918) that Hafod would have to be sold when he died,

The mansion, photographed in 1941 by George Tarrant, son of the then owner.

J. Macve

Waddingham's motivation for investing in the estate's future was diminished, and after his wife's death in 1910 he became something of a recluse. The estate was reduced in size in 1929 when over 5,000 acres of upland in the north-east, including much of what had been Johnes's experimental farm, were leased to the Forestry Commission, and in 1933 a further 3,000 acres were rented to the University of Wales, later being sold to MAFF and becoming what is now the research farm of ADAS Pwllpeiran.

When T.J. Waddingham died in 1938, at the age of 98, the outlook for the Hafod estate was very uncertain. In 1939, as war loomed, John Piper visited Hafod as part of a tour of threatened buildings, and his photographs and drawings captured the house and landscape in the early stages of decay, romantic but still rescuable. In the following year it was bought by W.G. Tarrant, a timber merchant and master builder from Surrey. Although possessed of ambitions to restore the house and make the estate a flourishing concern, Tarrant was short of money and started the process of extensive clear-felling, justified by the demands of the war effort. He also made strenuous efforts to interest the Ministry of Supply in Hafod's mining potential, and opened up some of the old levels on Allt Dihanog. One substantial landscape feature was created: the barrage across the river at Dologau which supplied hydro-electric power to the house, estate cottages and buildings. Tarrant, who was the last to use the mansion as a permanent home, died suddenly in 1942, and subsequently Hafod was owned by a succession of timber merchants. With each change of ownership the estate was reduced in size, as farms and cottages were sold to tenants, until in 1950 most of the demesne – by now almost denuded of trees – and some outlying areas were acquired for the Forestry Commission.

The early years of the Forestry Commission's custodianship of Hafod were not happy ones. Dense softwood plantations appeared on the sides and floor of the Ystwyth valley, where formerly there had been mixed woodland or open meadow, and surviving old broadleaves found themselves hemmed in by fast-growing conifers. To facilitate forestry operations, a concrete bridge was erected across the river in the heart of the demesne, and new roads made on either side,

obliterating some lengths of old path and part of the Flower Garden. Historic built features, such as the Alpine Bridge, were allowed to decay. A seasonal caravan site – fondly recalled by Caravan Club members who stayed there – was established in the field around the mansion ruins. All remaining estate houses were sold, with the exception of Hawthorn Cottage.

THE HAFOD PROJECT

In the 1980s there was increasing public awareness and concern for Hafod, and a local voluntary society, the Friends of Hafod, was formed. This, combined with the presence of a sympathetic forest manager and availability of limited public funding for restoration, gave rise to a scheme for opening up and restoring parts of the demesne. Two new trails were created, almost entirely along the routes of old estate paths, the Flower Garden and Mariamne's Garden were cleared and their walls and gateways rebuilt, and the Bedford Monument restored. In 1989 a new charitable body, the Welsh Historic Gardens Trust, came into being and soon afterwards plans for a more extensive programme of work at Hafod began to take shape. Following a generous offer of grant aid for Hafod from a private benefactor, the Trust entered into negotiations with the Forestry Commission, and in 1992 the Hafod Heritage Partnership Agreement was signed.

Following documentary and field research and discussions with interested parties, plans were drawn up for restoration of the two main walks described by George Cumberland in *An Attempt to Describe Hafod*. Work began on establishing and reconstructing a section of the First or Lady's Walk, from the Flower Garden to the church, while Forest Enterprise (part of the Forestry Commission) began the gradual process of restoring the landscape by clear-felling or thinning plantations along the route of the walk. A detailed archaeological survey of the Alpine Bridge was carried out, in preparation for its rebuilding. In 1994, the Welsh Historic Gardens Trust transferred its responsibilities for the Hafod project to the newly formed Hafod Trust, which continued the work in progress and fund-raising. In 1996 the restored Alpine Bridge was opened and a bicentenary edition of *An Attempt to Describe Hafod* was published by the Hafod Trust. In the following year two circuit walks, incorporating newly restored sections, were opened and a guide leaflet produced.

In 1998 a successful application was made to the Heritage Lottery Fund. This enabled the Hafod Partnership (i.e. The Forestry Commission and Hafod Trust) to employ a full-time estate manager and other staff, to provide a permanent office base on site by converting the Waddingham stables, and to continue work on restoration of the path network and other historic features. It also funded further surveys and interpretative research, providing a deeper understanding of the structure of the landscape, the views within it and historical plantings and land-use. This knowledge is being used to enhance and implement the forest design and devise sensitive management schemes. Only very limited areas remain to be clear-felled, with the future emphasis elsewhere being on gradual thinning and the introduction of broadleaved woodland, and on the improvement of existing open spaces.

In 2001-2003, substantial funding from Cydcoed, the Headley Trust, and a private donor, enabled further capital works to be carried out. Hawthorn Cottage, which had been empty for many years and was slipping towards dereliction, was leased from FC by the Hafod Trust and fully restored. The walks network was extended, with the completion of the Ystwyth Gorge Walk, the Coed Hafod Walk, and the Garden Walk. The Partnership also co-operated with Ceredigion County Council by funding and initiating repairs (including a new board walk) on the public footpath that enters the estate from Pontrhydygroes along the south bank of the Ystwyth.

Photo: Phil Smith

The Alpine Bridge, from upstream

THE HAFOD WALKS

BACKGROUND

Within the estate there are some 15 km (8-9 miles) of paths available to walkers, and with a few exceptions they follow historical routes. The distances given are for the length of the walk from its starting place to its end, but note that not all walks start at the car park and therefore additional distances may be involved. All walks described here are way-marked. There is also a network of public rights-of-way at Hafod, but these are described only when they coincide with a way-marked path. A walkers' leaflet, with large-scale map and explanatory text, is available separately and grades the routes according to their level of difficulty. The following section aims to describe the walks in their landscape and historical context. Although it may have been possible to reach some of the main features at Hafod in a small carriage (with a short walk at the end), the landscape was designed to be enjoyed on foot, enabling the visitor gradually to be drawn under its spell and appreciate its intricacies. The Rev. Richard Warner described the walks as:

commanding views beautiful, romantic, and astonishing; woods and rocks; bridges and cataracts; the highly-ornamented garden, and the rude, rugged, uncultivated mountain.

This hints at the variety to be found, both in the subject matter and the scale of views. One moment one might be pausing to admire an intimate view of a glade of oaks or a small cascade over a rock, the next one might come to an opening that revealed a grand panorama down the valley. George Cumberland placed eighteen stars on his map to mark the "fine points of View",

Photo: J. Macve

The chain bridge and Ystwyth gorge

A viewpoint on the Garden Walk. Its supporting stone revetment was restored in 2003.

but many more viewpoints have been identified from other sources or on the ground. Most lie on the path routes, though some require a short diversion; many take advantage of natural features but others have clearly been constructed as platforms. Landforms or vegetation were used in places to conceal the view until the walker arrived at the viewpoint, and to shape and contain the view itself. Those visitors with an eye attuned to the Picturesque would have known how to read the landscape through these views and perhaps to use the viewpoints as sketching stations – assisted by Johnes's practice of placing "convenient seats in eligible situations".

That Johnes considered the experience of walking through the landscape of prime importance is evident from the fact that the two main walks had been completed by 1787, within four years of his arrival at Hafod and notwithstanding the distractions of building a new house at the same time. There are no records of how Johnes went about the practical task of designing and constructing the paths, other than visitors' descriptions and the physical remains themselves. Cumberland gives a brief description of their structure:

[the walks] are all dry, kept clean, and composed of materials found on the spot; …. few are steep; the transitions easy, the returns commodious, and the branches distinct. … all that is here done, has been to remove obstructions, reduce the materials, and conceal the art.

"Concealing the art" was most important: the finished result should look as natural and uncontrived as possible. Although some of the images by John "Warwick" Smith imply a rather formal appearance, this may have been a stylistic device to emphasise the presence of the walks. Evidence from other contemporary estates and writings suggests that the paths would have been low-key with gentle curves and irregular, indistinct edges, so that one was not distracted from the surroundings by the line of the walk itself. Traces of foundations and surfaces revealed by archaeology show a fairly constant width of about one metre, but can give no indication of how vegetation may have been used to soften the line. Where walks traversed steep slopes – which in many places they do – the need to cut into the soil or rock dictated a fairly narrow, regular width. It is these hillside terrace paths that have survived best, and in restoring them the Partnership has tried to preserve their natural appearance: angling them slightly into the slope and sometimes forming a berm on the outer edge to make them less visible from a distance; using natural materials for revetments or, in a few places where concrete is called for, concealing it; and keeping safety rails to a minimum. Some of the first sections of walk to be restored were surfaced throughout with stone chippings, but later this was used sparingly and only where muddy conditions demanded it. Elsewhere bark was laid to establish a line in fairly level terrain, but for much of the path network it was found that no surfacing material was needed.

The Rev. William Gilpin (who had not actually visited Hafod) referred to "the lady's-walk, a circuit of about three miles – and the gentleman's-walk, about six." He may have had those terms (and rather exaggerated distances) from Johnes himself, and for convenience they are used today.

Cumberland, who calls them simply the First and Second Walks, is the only writer to describe the entire original circuits in detail. We know from Johnes's letters, later descriptions, maps, and evidence on the ground that he created other walks, but on the whole detailed accounts of the routes and illustrations are lacking. We also know that by about 1800 the extent of walks available to visitors had been reduced. This may have been due to changes in land management – Johnes wishing to avoid sending walkers through, say, a young plantation or a ploughed field – or it may have been to do with the logistics of managing visitors. Close friends of Johnes could stay for two weeks or more as a guest at the mansion, giving ample time to explore different routes, but those lodging at the Hafod Arms might allow only one day for Hafod. The usual pattern was for visitors to arrive from Devil's Bridge by post-chaise and begin by viewing the interior of the house. They might then take a look at the kitchen garden before being conducted by the gardener along the north bank of the river to the flower garden. From there, if in a hurry, they could simply follow the Lady's Walk to the Peiran Falls and then to Upper Lodge where their post-chaise awaited them. Others found time to ascend to the south to see the Cavern Cascade, or explore the Ystwyth Gorge, or possibly both, but this still left much of the south and west of the demesne unvisited. A few tourists, in their haste to get round Wales, neglected Hafod altogether and contented themselves with some brisk scrambling around the falls at Devil's Bridge.

George Cumberland and Sir James Edward Smith both described with great enthusiasm the scenery of the Ystwyth valley just west of Hafod, which also features on some of the Crown Derby Hafod Service dishes. Known as Coed Maenarthur, this wooded gorge was part of the Earl of Lisburne's Crosswood estate. Its spectacular views and cascades were equal to anything at Hafod, and it is probable that Johnes hoped to acquire it: indeed, it is unlikely that he would have encouraged his friends to explore and describe it if this were not his objective. No such transfer of ownership took place, however, and later visitors were not directed towards Maenarthur. Today its woods are accessible from Pontrhydygroes via the Miners' Bridge (rebuilt in 2002), and a way-marked trail of 3 km links up old paths and affords views of the gorge and valley, Grogwynion hill fort, and relict industrial features.

Photo: Phil Smith

The Lady's Walk beside the Ystwyth

THE LADY'S WALK
(3.6 km/2.2 miles - Blue Route)

The Lady's Walk is a circular route around the north-eastern part of the demesne; it does not cross the river at any point. The walk passed through very varied scenery but with none of the wilderness atmosphere of the Gentleman's Walk. There were no caves, precipices, or steep slopes, and a visit to the formal flower garden was included. George Cumberland walked it in an anti-clockwise direction, starting from the house.

The walk crossed the front "lawn" – a term used then to describe a piece of meadow, rather than something purely ornamental. The original route approached the Alpine Bridge before turning left along the riverbank, where it soon narrowed to a ledge, but to date restoration of this path to a satisfactory standard has proved prohibitively expensive, owing to the presence of an old spoil dump and erosion by the river making the slope unstable. An alternative route, shown on Cumberland's map, is used instead. After passing through the rock cutting (the probable source of the spoil) it follows Johnes's drive along the top of the slope before turning down a side track to re-join the riverside route near the site of the Cold Bath. This small building, consisting of a plunge pool and dressing-room and fed by a spring, was mentioned by several early visitors to Hafod, but is absent from later records and may well have been demolished by Johnes in his later years. Its site was

Photo: Cambria Archaeology

Entrance to the Cold Bath, during its excavation in 1998

excavated in 1998, and the remains of the walls (faced with oolitic limestone), flooring, entrance steps and a culvert were uncovered, but then back-filled.

From the Cold Bath one can now take the Garden Walk (see p.38) to the left, but Cumberland continued down the track to emerge on to a meadow, which, he said, "conveys an idea of warm, screened, and solitary retirement". Visually enclosed by steep wooded hills, this open space was at the heart of the landscape and visible from overviews. John "Warwick" Smith showed a small herd of cows grazing on it – perhaps turned out here after a hay crop had been cut. In the 1950s it was planted with Lodgepole pines but, after clear-felling in 1994, grass regenerated well and views in all directions were suddenly revealed. To restore

NLW

Meadow below the Flower Garden: aquatint by Stadler after J. Smith. (1810)

Photo: Phil Smith

Cascade of the Peiran, at its junction with the Ystwyth

the tradition of grazing and prevent growth of scrub, it has been fenced and is grazed at certain times of year by a few Welsh Black cattle. Originally the Lady's Walk hugged the inside edge of the meadow, passing under some rock outcrops, but this route is absent from later maps and may have been superseded by the Garden Walk above. For those wishing to enjoy close-up views of the river, an alternative path runs along its bank outside the cattle fence.

Turning out of the meadow at its upper end, the walker should enjoy a fine view along the next stretch of river, but this is now sadly interrupted by a 1960s road bridge. To the left of it lies Mrs Johnes's Flower Garden (see under "Garden Walk", below). The path follows a narrowing strip of ground that become a ledge; the rocky river-bed and the gnarled mossy trees overhanging it are notably picturesque. Sections of this path had fallen into the river and have been rebuilt with revetments. Having rounded another river bend, the walk approaches a barrier, Nant Peiran, otherwise known as the mill stream, which forms a pretty cascade as it joins the river. On the opposite bank of the stream (across a neat, Johnes-built stone bridge) is the former estate sawmill, built by William Chambers in the 1860s and still in use in the 1940s but now a private house. Leaving the river behind, the walk ascends into the woods, keeping close to the stream, which here runs over steeply inclined rock strata in chutes and swirls.

The walk now approaches its visual climax, the Peiran Falls. Cumberland's description, with a bridge, a rocky pass, steps, and walls in a rapid sequence, is confused and may be inaccurate: Johnes afterwards told him (out of tact perhaps) that he proposed to "change the walk over the Millbrook, to make it correspond with your description". What is clear is that there was a small summerhouse or covered seat here (referred to now as the Rustic Alcove), and that the path was so designed that the building and other features blocked the view of the falls until one emerged on the other side. This arrangement may have been modified by the Duke of Newcastle, and all that now remains is, to the left, the rear wall of the Alcove and on the right a low wall that once formed part of a bridge abutment. Ahead is the cascade, falling in two stages and with a massive, slanting rock in front. Historical images generally show the lower fall dividing in two to pass either side of this rock; in periods of very wet weather this effect is recreated and the whole stream becomes a dramatic flume of white water. Cumberland reports that he once saw the cascade at night lit by Bengal Fire – an early form of floodlighting, made from black sulphide of antimony.

Leaving the falls, the walk turns sharp left and climbs on a gently rising terrace, through what in 1794 was an old woodland of outgrown coppiced oaks, grazed by sheep, but is now a stand of mature Noble and Grand Firs. The "sound of the wave", as Cumberland says, "ascends with you".

NLW

Photo: Phil Smith

The upper Peiran Falls

Photo: Phil Smith

The Peiran Falls

a new plantation) described by Cumberland. The line taken by the restored path was the "best fit" that could be found in 1994, but is too uneven in gradient to be a true representation of the original. It is hoped, however, that at least the view across the valley can be recreated in time as conifers below are thinned out. At the top of a steep climb, the path joins a broad, terraced walk that is believed to be later than, and probably overlies, the Lady's Walk. It may have been intended as a route from the drive to the church suitable for a governess cart, but its lower end was never completed.

Arriving at the church, Cumberland commented on its site, "niched in a wood" with ancient yews around it, but gave no description of the church itself, which at that time had not yet been rebuilt by Johnes (see p.51). He then turned for home and gave a brief account of a section of path for which there are no other witnesses. Although it may have crossed the summit of the ridge, Cefn Creigiau, the fact that no views are described makes it more likely that it followed the line of the

The path crosses the 1813 carriage drive (see Ystwyth Gorge Walk, below) and a short distance beyond comes to the main drive from Upper Lodge. The next section of walk was problematic, all trace of the original having disappeared, along with the viewpoint and the fence (perhaps around

Photo: Eric Thomas

Hawthorn Cottage and the pond

modern track, staying close to the upper edge of the woodland. The craggy top of the hill, until recently densely planted with conifers, has been cleared to recreate the rough pasture of Johnes's time. The far end of the ridge, where Cumberland reached a rocky promontory commanding fine views, was greatly altered by Johnes over the next few years - an encircling wall was built, Mariamne's Garden and Pen-creigiau cottage constructed, and some seven acres planted, mainly with larch – and the walk may have been closed or re-routed as a result. Later the plateau became criss-crossed with a bewildering number of paths, rides, and timber extraction tracks. The restored walk takes the most logical line through this network, with a loop to what is believed to be Cumberland's viewpoint, and then zigzags down the west face of the ridge.

The final leg of the walk is across open ground, former hay meadows that happily were kept free of later planting and are now under organic grazing management. The path loops across Pendre meadow and passes below a group of private houses on the site of Johnes's home farm, to arrive at a prettily composed picturesque scene: Hawthorn Cottage (known before 1850 as Pendre Isaf) and Pendre pond, lying in a sheltered hollow. Cumberland's map shows two ponds here, but no trace of the long pond has been found. Both may have originated as fish ponds, and the surviving pond was where Johnes had a "menagerie" –

apparently containing nothing more exotic than guinea-fowl and peacocks. The one-storey dairyman's cottage was rebuilt in the late 19th century by John Waddingham into its present form, and was restored and made habitable by the Hafod Trust in 2002. In the following year the pond was cleaned out, with the help of student volunteers, and pipes were laid to re-establish its water supply. Beyond it the Lady's Walk reappears strongly as a terrace on the side of Middle Hill, from where the mansion would have been suddenly in view for the first time since the start of the walk.

The Garden Walk and Flower Garden

The Garden Walk is a later modification of the Lady's Walk, running above the Ystwyth meadow instead of through it. Although not in existence at the time of Cumberland's visit, it is referred to by a later commentator as "a walk through the woods" from the flower garden, and has the physical characteristics of a Johnes path. Before restoration its route was clearly traceable on the ground, and for most of its length only relatively minor constructional work was needed to reinstate it.

The walk leaves the main track at the site of the Cold Bath, climbs gently, and soon crosses a stream by means of a small wooden bridge placed on original stone abutments. It then winds along the hillside, hugging the contours of the ground. In due course it meets a bluff of rock rising vertically from the meadow, and here several ledges have been cut to form a tiered viewpoint, from which views of the river and opposite hills could be enjoyed. The walk itself is supported by a stone revetment, carefully restored in 2003. Beyond this point the path descends gradually on to a wide terrace above the meadow, before arriving at the flower garden.

The flower garden was in existence by 1788, when Jane Johnes referred to it as "my flower garden" – hence its alternative name of Mrs Johnes's Garden. Although we have no detailed descriptions or plans of it, it appears to have shown strongly the influence of William Mason's poem *The English Garden*, being a glade,
circled by shade, yet pervious to the sun
with flowers arranged in plots,
… interpos'd between the wand'ring lines
of shaven turf which twisted to the path…
[that] stole round the verdant limits of the scene.

The Piper Estate / Richard Broyd

Gateway in the Flower Garden, with satyr's head keystone:
watercolour by John Piper (1939)

The perimeter wall enclosed a space of just over one acre, though a deceptive sense of space misled Cumberland and others to describe it as being two acres in size. There was a deliberate contrast between the formality of the garden and the woodland and river scenery outside it, and unlike Mariamne's private garden, it was intended to be visited and admired by picturesque tourists. It contained a small summerhouse in the form of a temple, perhaps at the highest part with a view out to the river, and a triton statue or fountain made of Coade stone. The same artificial stone was applied to the two gateways as voussoirs and keystones, possibly at the suggestion of John Nash. American shrubs and trees, which were collectors' items and status symbols to eighteenth century landowners, were planted in the garden, and as these matured it may have taken on a less formal appearance.

The garden today contains almost no surface features to give clues to its layout, and only one tree, a holm oak, that may be original. It was the worst casualty of forestry developments in the mid-twentieth century, when it was subsumed into a plantation and had an access road, on an ugly embankment, driven through it. In the 1980s its wall and gates were repaired, with replica Coade stone ornamentation (though the two heads are not accurate representations of the original nymph and satyr). Various means of re-routing the road have been discussed, but to do this would inevitably mean destroying another piece of landscape. As long as lorry access is needed through the estate, the road remains a necessary evil. At the time of writing ways are being considered of improving the garden in a manner that would be sympathetic to its history and provide a more interesting space for the public.

The walk crosses the garden and leaves by the east gate. Here the ground has been built up – probably to accommodate an earlier timber extraction track that passed north of the garden wall – and the line of the old path has been lost. Its modern replacement descends a bank and joins the Lady's Walk beside the river.

THE GENTLEMAN'S WALK
(6 km / 3.7 miles - Red Route)

The Gentleman's Walk is a circular route through much wilder scenery and steeper ground than the Lady's Walk. It shows Thomas Johnes at the height of his powers as a landscape designer, and embodies the spirit of the Picturesque at Hafod in its purest form.

The walk began at the Alpine Bridge, reached by a path branching off the track to the kitchen garden. Today a short diversion from this route takes in the icehouse. Believed to have been built by Johnes, this little structure is made entirely of stone rather than the more usual brick – which would have been difficult and expensive to obtain in this remote place before the coming of the railways. Its deep well and vaulted roof survive, though the entrance tunnel has gone save for some low sidewalls. Ice was collected from estate ponds and also perhaps from the river by submerging wooden trays in the shallows, but if these supplies were insufficient it may also have been brought in from overseas.

The eighteenth-century perception of an "Alpine" bridge was a rustic wooden structure carried at some height above a rocky torrent. The first known bridge here, which may have pre-dated Johnes, matched this description, being nothing more elaborate than some tree trunks supported in the middle by a stone pier. Johnes rebuilt it at least once, replacing its rude simplicity with an innovative design of two wooden arches, which was variously described as elegant and Moorish by visitors, and as the "Bridge of Sighs" on a sale map. By the early twentieth century its pier and abutments had been raised to their present height and the deck was a simple timber span. This was used as the model for the reconstruction of the bridge, which necessitated substantial reinforcement and repair of the stonework as well as a completely new deck.

The bridge conveys the walker abruptly from open parkland into shady woodland. Mature beeches overhang a junction of paths; three public rights-of-way diverge from here, including, to the right, a riverside walk to Pontrhydygroes. The Gentleman's Walk takes the fourth option, climbing gently to the left. The width and contoured curves are untypical of the walk as a whole, and may be a later modification to accommodate small vehicles. The path enters a plantation of Western Hemlock – intrusive or atmospheric, depending on one's view of the gloomy tunnel created – and is then cut across by a track, deepened by timber extraction. The walk crosses this and descends on a narrow terrace into the dingle of Nant Bwlchgwallter. After crossing what appears to be a dry waterfall – perhaps a failed or incomplete piece of Johnes water

Photo: Phil Smith

*Rustic bridge across
Nant Bwlchgwallter*

engineering – it arrives at the stream and a viewpoint. Here there stood a "rustic shed" from which one could admire a cascade, Pistyll Dihanog (a recently coined name for a previously unnamed feature). Above is an arched road bridge, which although built in 1955, is so weathered and in shadow as to be inoffensive, and confines the view quite neatly. There may have been an earlier bridge on the same site.

The viewpoint and opposite bank have been eroded by the stream, so that the original crossing point of Johnes's log footbridge – and a later metal suspension bridge whose anchor points survive – is no longer viable. Instead a rustic bridge has been built a short way downstream at a rocky narrows, and from here steps lead up to rejoin the Gentleman's Walk. Having rounded a ridge and levelled out, the route becomes speculative, as its historical line could be traced only in a few fragments before disappearing beneath the modern forest road. Shortly before this, a viewpoint among tumbled rocks and old oak stumps overlooks the river and meadow below.

For some distance the walk now unavoidably follows the forest road. After 250m some steps on the right lead to the "short-cut", a Johnes path that can be used to by-pass the circuit of Dologau fields. The route taken by George Cumberland continues down the road to the river bend; here he remarked on a group of ash trees and a gate leading out of the forest, just beyond which was a fine view down the valley (not up, as he mistakenly says). The view remains, but planting and road-building have destroyed the little open space here and obliterated the "straight path" (perhaps carried on an embankment to avoid wet ground). Steps and a stile carry the walk into Dologau fields, which are managed by ADAS Pwllpeiran research farm. The line of beeches on the right, together with trees on the riverbank, formed the "front screen" referred to by Cumberland: when he looked back from the top of the fields, they concealed the river and thus delayed the grandest view to a later part of the walk. On the opposite bank is the Lady's Walk, and Nant Peiran can be seen cascading into the river.

After passing through a small piece of woodland, from which the impressive stone arch of Dologau bridge can be seen, one reaches a track. Straight ahead the Ystwyth Gorge Walk begins, crossing a footbridge over a rushing stream (Nant Gau), but the Gentleman's Walk turns right, makes a short diversion from the original route to avoid a private house and then continues along the lower edge of the next field.

Re-entering the forest, the walk meets Nant Gau again, and encounters a well-preserved section of ditch. This was a leat that led from a pool on the stream (retained by a dam that has not survived) and was part of Johnes's water management scheme, whereby meadows were "floated" or "drowned" by means of stream-water diverted across them, to improve the soil's fertility and moisture content. A rock-cut ledge carries the path along the stream, past a waterfall and narrow ravine, through "the most romantic scenery". Climbing away from the stream for a short distance, the walk arrives at a junction by a grove of large beech trees. Sharp right is the return route of the Gentleman's Walk, but those with a taste for the Sublime, and energy for an extended walk, should skirt round the fallen beech and continue up the valley, on an unmarked public footpath. For the first 50m the path departs from its historical

Photo: Eilish Carr

A beech at Pant Melyn

41

The Cavern Cascade after a hard frost

line, being blocked by a landslip, and passes instead through a ruined wall, turns left, and drops down a steep slope to re-join the true route. One path then branches left across a bridge and heads for Cwmystwyth, but the Gentleman's Walk continues up the same bank of the stream.

Within this deep valley, where ancient semi-natural woodland survives, the path twists and climbs to reveal a succession of picturesque views of cascading water and deep pools amongst rocks and mossy trees. In one place the stream forces its way through a narrow opening and falls vertically into a wide pool, marking a zone of weakness on the line of a geological fault; in the hope of finding a rich mineral seam within it, miners have at some date excavated a trial level to the right of the path. Further small cascades and chutes are passed before one sees another stream joining Nant Gau from the opposite bank and spreading out across a near-vertical slab of rock in a mare's-tail, or "pisse-vache" to use Cumberland's term (recalling a famous waterfall in the Swiss Alps). Finally the path comes to a stop in front of a dark opening in the hillside, and the walker must negotiate a low rock-climb and an unlit tunnel to reach the

celebrated Cavern Cascade. Numerous writers and a few artists have tried to convey the experience of discovering the cascade, but it is probably best to leave the visitor to derive their own surprise and delight at it.

Cumberland describes a bridge across the stream below the cave entrance, and Johnes later built a walk down the opposite side, but neither bridge nor walk survive. The Gentleman's Walk therefore retraces its steps to the junction in the beech grove, where it keeps left to begin its circuit of a domed hill, known historically as Bryn Tyloge. Cumberland's imagination was so excited by the shape of this "globose promontory" and its central position in the landscape that he proposed to Johnes that a "druid temple" (i.e. a stone circle) should be placed upon it. Johnes received the idea favourably and Cumberland duly marked the temple on his map. But although Johnes made enquiries from an architect, Thomas Harrison of Chester, about a suitable design, there is no evidence that he took the matter any further.

Cumberland also devotes considerable time to describing the views that opened up as the walk

Cavern Cascade cave entrance

progressed around the hill: the church, the flower garden, and the Ystwyth river and vale stretching away to the west, with Grogwynion Falls visible 5 km away. His description (and that of B.H. Malkin a few years later) seems to imply that the crown of the hill was bare of trees, but early pictures and maps, as well as evidence from stumps and the surviving mature beeches, suggest at least scattered tree cover - perhaps wood pasture with carefully placed gaps between trees to allow views out. Future management will reflect this, with care being taken to protect the beeches from too much exposure to wind, whilst between them views are opened up from the path and from the top of the hill (to which an alternative path leads). Open space will be created in the col south of the hill (Pant Melyn), which was a small area of clear pasture in Johnes's time.

On the far side of the hill the walk crosses a track and soon reaches an old boundary bank. Here there was a noticeable change of landscape type, not experienced today, as it entered the dense cover of old estate woodlands. A short way below the path another bank and ditch mark the upper limit of a lost field, Cae Top, which in due course will be re-created. Within it was a small pond (awaiting restoration) which may have been another of Johnes's watering systems. The walk continues almost straight and level along a contour for 800m, with little to remark on in Cumberland's account other than deep foliage and occasional views out, including one near the junction with the "short-cut". Farther on the slope becomes steeper, obliging the path to cut into rock and ascend some steps, emerging on to a viewpoint. Before restoration the walk was blocked here by a fallen tree, but it proved possible to winch the trunk clear of the path and use it as a natural parapet wall. Rounding a corner one arrives suddenly at a cave-opening in a sheer rock face. From the platform in front of the cave the Bedford Monument is visible across the valley, appearing very small and giving a sense of great distance and depth. The walk passes through a tunnel, which has a corner within it to prevent a through-view and deepen the "poetical gloom", thus heightening the drama. The sound of falling water from somewhere below adds a further effect.

The tunnel on Allt Dihanog

 is labelled *Photo: Phil Smith*

 is labelled *Photo: Forest Life Picture Library*

Photo: Phil Smith

The Gentleman's Walk on a rock-cut ledge

The walk continues along the slope, through a scattered scree of mossy boulders, and crosses a track that originally led up to Johnes's "Alpine farm" at Bwlchgwallter. It then rounds a corner and is carried on a rock-cut ledge along the precipitous side of a narrow valley, down which Nant Bwlchgwallter rushes in a series of falls. At the crossing point for the walk the stream was, in Cumberland's time, divided into two branches (perhaps artificially) with an island between them; two stone-slab bridges crossed from either bank to the island, where the "Mossy Seat" provided a

resting point with a view of the falls above. The stream has now abandoned the west arm, and its wide single channel requires a more substantial bridge, carried high enough to avoid damage by flash floods. A jumble of large rocks is all that remains of the Mossy Seat, but whether they were once arranged into a more regular structure, perhaps with a simple roof, is not known. On the banks can be seen the metal supports of another vanished suspension bridge, similar to those directly downhill where the Gentleman's Walk crossed this same stream on its outward leg. The

NLW

Cascade above the Mossy Seat: aquatint by Stadler after J. Smith (1810)

construction of these bridges appears similar to Johnes's chain bridge in the gorge, but the finish is cruder and no visitors from his time refer to them, so it is assumed that they are the work of a later owner – perhaps John Waddingham. No drawings, photographs or descriptions of them have yet come to light.

The remainder of the Gentleman's Walk is described by no-one other than Cumberland. Shortly after crossing the bridge he had his first view of the mansion, "drop't like a pearl on the opposite sloping hill", since setting out. The path runs on a straight terrace but is soon interrupted by a forest road. A walk of about 200m up the road brings one to a bend and a wide view across the field of Cae Gwartheg to the hills beyond. Just to the right of the road is a hillock from which Cumberland enjoyed another fine prospect, with views of the house, the Ystwyth valley to the east, and the high sheepwalks above the woods. Current design plans for Hafod propose that this summit will be cleared to re-establish it as a viewpoint.

A public footpath descends steeply from the bend in the road through the beech woods to the Alpine Bridge. To follow Cumberland's route, however, we must continue along the track, though he gives us no information about topography or views and so we are reliant on his map and surface archaeology to guide us. The path branches right to leave the road and keeps along the upper edge of Cae Gwartheg. This field is being reclaimed for grazing and will be planted with loose clumps of trees, including sweet chestnut. One hundred and fifty years of successive planting and felling had destroyed much of the walk, but sufficient remained to reconstruct its route with some confidence. Turning at the top corner of the field, it keeps along the upper edge of the deep valley of Nant Ffin. Where the ground drops away, a branch path gives access to the stream's edge and a view of a cascade. The main path continues to the lower boundary of the field, where it descends steeply through woods to a junction with the Pontrhydygroes footpath. Cumberland's route crossed this and reached the Ystwyth, where he found a "very long flying bridge" to carry him across to the kitchen garden. There is no trace of any abutments for this bridge, and one suggestion is that it was in fact a boat, propelled by ropes and pulleys across a pool above a low dam; whatever its form, it seems to have been short-lived, as no other visitor referred to it or sketched it. The modern visitor must instead turn right and follow the path along the river to the Alpine Bridge.

Photo: Forest Life Picture Library

*The Hafod valley
from the
Gentleman's Walk*

THE YSTWYTH GORGE WALK
(1.5 km / 1 mile - Green Route)

This route takes the walker on a long, narrow loop up one side of the Ystwyth gorge and down the other. It connects with both the Lady's and Gentleman's Walks. Despite the dramatic scenery along the walk, the gradients are relatively gentle, but it is not a route suitable for those who dislike steep drops beside the path.

Both George Cumberland and Sir James Edward Smith describe a walk along the south side of the gorge, the latter informing us that it was called the New Walk, though at that date (mid-1790s) it was still unfinished. For once we are also provided with an insight into how Johnes went about designing the walk:

...this indefatigable enthusiast for the beauties of wild scenery undertook to wade at low water for a considerable extent along its bed, climbing over no trifling rocky impediments, and observing, as he went, where the happiest points of view might be chosen.
    Sir James Edward Smith, *A Tour to Hafod* , p.14

Thomas Johnes should perhaps be credited with inventing the sport of gorge walking.

It was to be another ten years before the walk was finished. Archaeological findings and descriptions by visitors suggest that it may have gone through various stages of development, with partly built sections abandoned in favour of a more exciting route. When finally completed in 1805, it was truly sublime, clinging to narrow ledges 10-20 ft above the water on both sides of the river. At its upstream end, the two arms of the walk were joined by a graceful "chain" bridge slung across a rocky chasm.

Today the original route of the New Walk can be traced, but for the most part it has not been restored for public use. The south arm has been badly affected by erosion, some sections having fallen into the river and others being compromised by landslips; the north arm, though in slightly better condition, is unacceptably hazardous in places. It was felt that introducing substantial revetments and guardrails would greatly detract from the sublime experience and wilderness atmosphere, as well as being a major challenge in engineering and financial terms. For the Ystwyth Gorge Walk a route has been devised at a higher level above the river, connecting up various old drives and paths with a few modern links.

Taking the clockwise route, the walk begins by branching off the Lady's Walk just where the latter

Photo: Phil Smith

The site of Pont Newydd on the east carriage drive

crosses the disused drive near the Peiran Falls. Johnes built this drive in the winter of 1813-14, when the weather was very severe and farm work impossible. As he explained to George Cumberland: *I found out a fine job for my poor labourers in the making of a new & most beautiful approach from Pentre [Cwmystwyth]. From 40 to 50 poor fellows never lost but two days at this work.*

The walk follows the drive and soon comes to Nant Peiran, where the original carriage-width bridge, Pont Newydd, has gone, though its massive stone abutments survive. No springing points for Johnes's two arches can be seen, and it appears that the Duke of Newcastle may have rebuilt the abutments when he installed a wooden deck braced from below by diagonal struts. By the 1980s, most of the superstructure had collapsed. Rather than replace it with a footbridge in the same position, it was decided to take the Ystwyth Gorge Walk a little way upstream, where there was evidence for a much older bridge. To reach it, the walk crosses a shallow dry ditch. This was built by Johnes in order to lead a spout of water into the Peiran Falls from the side, for a more picturesque effect. It is now blocked by the causeway leading to Pont Newydd, and its intake from the stream has been destroyed.

The new Peiran footbridge is constructed in the same way as the Mossy Seat bridge on the Gentleman's Walk, with one massive oak beam acting as both support and footway. From the bridge there are pleasingly contrasted views: upstream to a shallow bed of slanting rocks between low grassy banks, and downstream to a dark ravine plunging towards the cascade. On the opposite side the bridge ends near the site of the Peiran Mill, marked by a slight cut platform at the foot of a high bank – in fact, the dam of the millpond. The little wooden mill was still in existence in 1794 but disused, having been closed by its former owner, the Earl of Lisburne, in the 1760s. The pond and a section of the leat that fed it are visible in the field above. The walk now rejoins the carriage drive, which for the next 200m overlies a medieval road that ran past the mill. The Peiran Falls can be glimpsed down to the right.

Rounding a bend cut through rock, the drive and walk turn east to run parallel to the river, which can be heard far below in the gorge. This was an old hanger wood when Johnes acquired the land in 1790, and it retains some mature oaks and groups of beech near the river. It is now an awkward piece of the estate to manage, having no road access, and therefore to minimize disruption much of it is likely to be clear-felled, retaining only the broadleaves. It will then be replanted with species that would have been available to Johnes, but leaving some new open space. In what is currently dense forest above the drive is the site of an old farmstead, Cefn yr Esgair; Cumberland saw it from across the river in 1794, but Johnes then appears to have demolished it. It was the birthplace of the Rev. Thomas Jones (1752 - 1845) a promoter of the Welsh Bible and one of the founders of the British and Foreign Bible Society. When farmland opens up on the left, the walk leaves the drive and turns right towards the river. This broad path that sweeps down the slope was almost certainly made by Johnes, either as an early, unfinished walk or to provide an easier means of access to the chain bridge.

Photo: Forest Life Picture Library

The chain bridge

47

At the foot of the path we reach the restored chain bridge, so called because the original was described as consisting of a plank deck supported on three chains. No remnants of chains were found on site, only fragments of wire rope, possibly because the chains were replaced at an earlier rebuild or because the term "chain" was used loosely to mean a method of suspension that hung like a chain. It is more properly described as a stressed ribbon bridge – a primitive type of suspension bridge where the weight is carried by cables under the deck rather than above it – and it is of interest in being one of the oldest of this type known in Britain, and indeed Europe. Nothing is known of how Johnes came by the design, expertise, and materials to build the bridge, though he was acquainted with the engineer, Matthew Boulton, and with ironworkers through the Knight family. At first he intended to locate it farther upstream, but it would be hard to improve on its final position. When restoration was first considered it was thought that a completely new structure would have to be built, either within the remains of the old bridge or a short distance away, but when the original iron rock-anchors (three on each side of the river) were subjected to proof load tests, it was found that they were more than capable of carrying the weight of a new bridge. The pairs of ornamental cast iron columns and smaller posts are as found; they bear no load but guide the cables. Although built of modern materials, with manila netting as a concession to modern safety concerns, the bridge replicates the shape and feel of the original and is a perfect platform from which to admire the water-worn rocks and gullies of the gorge.

On the south bank, the walk now coincides with the New Walk and soon arrives at the Gothic Arcade. Given this name by the artist, John Piper, who in 1939 painted the only known image of it, this little building is something of an enigma. It is obviously positioned so as to command a view of the chain bridge and to be an "eye-catcher" in view from the bridge, but there is no unequivocal evidence that it was built by Johnes, and it could be much later. In 1939 its lintel and three pointed arches were intact, but by the 1980s all that remained were the two outer pillars, one of which was leaning badly. Conservation in 2003 stabilised these outer pillars and the low side-walls that adjoin them, and rebuilt the lower sections of the two smaller, inner pillars from identifiable fragments on the ground. Discussion is underway at the time of writing as to the most appropriate way of restoring the structure to its original height.

The path continues to follow the New Walk along its shelf for a short distance, before a modern link takes it up the slope to an old path at a higher level. Whether this was also a Johnes route is not clear but, once the New Walk became obstructed, it was the only means of reaching the Gothic Arcade and had been in use for many years before its restoration as part of the Ystwyth Gorge Walk. Previously it ran through a dense plantation, but

Photo: The Piper Estate / NLW

The Gothic Arcade and Ystwyth Gorge, portrayed by John Piper (1939)

Dologau Bridge

referred to in historical documents, though it formed the backdrop to numerous pictures of the house. It consisted of 80 acres of "in hand" woodland in Johnes's time, and in 1807 he made the unwelcome decision to fell the entire wood to help finance the rebuilding of the mansion. He expected the timber to fetch a good price, as imports had been hit by a French embargo on British ships entering European ports. At first he considered thinning the woodland, but noted that complete clearance would "prevent any damage to the adjoining trees ... and will be more easily inclosed for replanting". Despite this justification on silvicultural grounds, he clearly feared criticism, saying: "when I plant so much yearly I think I have a right to fall [sic] what is in a decaying state". Johnes soon replanted, but successive owners felled and restocked, with John Waddingham introducing large areas of conifer plantation, and by 1950 the hillside was almost devoid of trees apart from a few timber oaks. The Forestry Commission planted beech, red oak, Japanese larch, Douglas fir and other conifers, which have been comprehensively thinned in recent years.

thinning has opened up good views into the gorge and up to the rocky summit of Cnwc Penpompren, while farther along, more distant views down the valley are revealed. As the path slopes down through larches, the concrete dam built by W.G. Tarrant is visible on the right, and beyond it, Dologau Bridge. The path then converges again with the line of the New Walk as it arrives at a footbridge across Nant Gau. Straight across the track is the Gentleman's Walk leading through fields to the concrete road bridge, from where there is a choice of routes back to the church car park.

Various tracks and paths ran up the slope to give access to the wood itself and to the parish road and farms above, and some are still in use. The Coed Hafod Walk crosses them at right-angles, running along the hillside in a similar way to the Gentleman's Walk across the valley. Despite this design, and the presence of certain features such as viewpoints and a stream engineered to branch in two, it is not recorded in documentary sources as a Johnes path. The earliest evidence for a walk along the hill comes from the Ordnance Survey plan of 1888, which shows a path starting from Pendre and climbing gently through the woods but then ending abruptly at a Waddingham plantation fence. There is evidence on the ground that it continued to climb and entered what are now privately owned fields. This mapped route, which was traceable on the ground for much of its length, forms the basis for the eastern half of the walk. To the west it has been built on the line of an old, worn path as far as a grand viewpoint, which looks out to Cae Gwartheg, Tŷ Coch, and the hills behind Pontrhydygroes. The final stretch of path, descending gently through a steep beech wood to the drive, is a new route.

COED HAFOD WALK

(1.2 km / 0.75 mile, one way - Brown Route)

This walk was reconstructed in 2003 as part of the Cydcoed-funded programme to improve community access to woodlands. It can be reached by walkers entering the estate from the west at Pontrhydygroes, from the north near Pantymawn, or from the church car park via Pendre track. It is not a circular route, and walkers must therefore decide on a return route to their starting place, using other walks or estate drives.

Coed Hafod, the steep, south-facing hillside along the northern side of the demesne, is seldom

Once on the drive, one can walk a short way up it and take a path to the left that cuts down to the

Lower Lodge Drive, which is rarely used by vehicles. This makes for a pleasant walk back towards the mansion fields, where the Lady's Walk can be followed to the car park at the church.

The Coed Hafod Walk passes through different woodland types, supporting a great variety of wildlife. In spring it is colourful with bluebells and azaleas. Its topography is relatively gentle – there are some rock outcrops but no caves or grand waterfalls – but the views from it to the river, the mansion fields and pond, and to distant hills are very fine and give a sense of discovering the landscape anew.

BEDFORD MONUMENT WALK
(1.6 km / 1 mile - Yellow Route)

The Bedford Monument Walk was opened in 1997 while the Lady's Walk was still undergoing restoration. Although it has no provenance as an historical circuit, it has been retained because it offers a short, relatively easy walk from the church, giving good views over the parkland.

The walk passes the rear gate of the churchyard and then takes the upper path, to the right. The style of this path suggests that it was almost certainly built by Johnes as a walk through the estate

woodlands to the church. It descends gently down the south-east side of Cefn Creigiau ridge, with peep views out to Dologau fields and beyond. Before reaching the main drive, the walk leaves this path by branching right and climbs in a zig-zag past rock outcrops to emerge on to a platform. From here there are superb views down the valley and across to the Gentleman's Walk. Perched on the edge of a precipice is the Bedford Monument, a classical stone obelisk designed by William F. Pocock and installed here in 1805. The column was restored in 1988 but the delicate inscription in marble was left untouched for fear of damaging it. It reads:

> To the memory of the most Noble Francis, late Duke of Bedford. This Obelisk is erected by Thomas Johnes, as a testimony of the sincerity with which he, in common with every friend to the Improvement of the Country, laments the loss of that most judicious and munificent promoter of the national Agriculture.

The 5th Duke (1765-1802) was a friend of Johnes and a fellow enthusiast for making agricultural improvements to his estates. After his death in 1802, his fiancée, Lady Georgiana Gordon,

The Bedford Monument

In Mariamne's Garden

married his brother John, the 6th Duke, and the couple visited Hafod in 1803.

A flight of stone steps climbs the steep crag behind the Monument to the gate into Mariamne Johnes's Garden (see p.21), which at the time of writing is awaiting restoration. Other than the outline of paths and steps it contains nothing from Mariamne's time, though some unusual trees – a grafted buck-eye and two Japanese hibas – are of interest.

From the Monument the walk proceeds down the slope, then turns right to follow an old estate path along the boundary of Pendre meadow. At a stile it crosses the Lady's Walk and continues straight on, now on a path built in 1988. The craggy top of Cefn Creigiau appears above, and there are views across the meadow to Middle Hill, Hawthorn Cottage, the pond, and the former bailiff's house at Pendre. The walk emerges on to Pendre drive near the site of Johnes's old lodge, Arch Uchaf, and follows the drive up to the right to arrive back at the car park.

THE CHURCH OF EGLWYS NEWYDD
dedicated to St Michael and All Angels

Historically the Hafod estate was spread across four parishes with the greatest part, north of the Ystwyth and including the house, falling within the parish of Upper Llanfihangel y Creuddyn. This was served by a church at Llantrisant, some 4.5 km (3 miles) from Hafod by the shortest route along windswept tracks. Once Hafod church had been built, Llantrisant fell out of use and then into dereliction, but was restored in 1883.

The first Egwlys Newydd (new church) at Hafod was built in 1620 by the then owner of Hafod, Morgan Herbert, to serve the growing community of the upper Ystwyth valley and for the convenience of his own household. Nothing now remains of this church other than its foundation stone, which is set into the outside wall beneath the altar window. The old font used to stand outside the main door but was stolen in 1989. George Cumberland tells us that the church had a "decent churchyard and ancient yews about it", but another early visitor (William Williams, 1796) found it to have a "mean and squalid appearance … [with] neither gate nor fence to the churchyard", and that inside "the floor was covered in dirt and weeds and from appearances it seemed to give occasional shelter to the cattle".

Thomas Johnes wished to have a more elegant adjunct to his estate, and appears to have at first reached agreement with the parish to share the expense of a new church, but as visitors like Mr Williams began to arrive and pass critical comment, he became impatient with delays and went ahead on his own. The chosen architect was James Wyatt, best known as the restorer of Salisbury cathedral and designer of extravagantly Gothic country houses. The church was built in 1801-2, and its outward appearance has changed little since then, though originally its tower was topped by a small steeple. An unusual feature of the layout is that the "east" window in fact faces south-west. The font, made of Coade stone, is decorated with carved roses, the Johnes arms, and figures representing the cardinal virtues. One window contained sixteenth-century Flemish stained glass brought over from the Low Countries by Johnes during the French Revolution, and over the altar was a painting by Fuseli of Christ and two disciples at Emmaus.

Burials for all three members of the Johnes family are recorded in the parish register, though none actually died at Hafod. All were buried in a family vault – built against what was then the west wall of the churchyard – and after Jane's burial the vault was sealed. A beautiful marble memorial to

51

Mariamne, sculpted by Sir Francis Chantrey after a drawing by Thomas Stothard, had been ordered and made during Johnes's lifetime but not fully paid for, and it was only in 1840 that it was finally brought from London and installed in the church, at the Duke of Newcastle's expense. It was considered one of Chantrey's finest works, and drew many visitors. The Duke also carried out some unspecified alterations to the church, which he regarded as a key component of the landscape. Further changes were made by the Waddingham family, who added a vestry, removed the gallery from above the door, and redecorated the interior. They were instrumental in providing Hafod with a vicarage (the vicar having previously lived in a house near the bridge at Pontrhydygroes and then at Pwllpeiran) and a schoolroom, and in 1894 they extended the churchyard to the west by incorporating a piece of estate woodland. James and Sarah Waddingham are buried beneath a white granite cross on the opposite side of the path to the Johnes grave. The churchyard was further extended, to the east, in the mid-twentieth century.

On Sunday 24th April 1932 the church was gutted by fire. It had just undergone repairs, including installation of electric light and a new heating system, and it appears that the fire originated in the vestry, where the stove had been lit in preparation for the first service for several months. The nearest telephone by which to summon help was in Devil's Bridge, and by the time the fire brigade had arrived from Aberystwyth the roof had already fallen in. In the meantime the vicar and caretaker had removed what they could from the burning building: the candlesticks, communion silver, altar cross, registers, and the oak doors were all rescued, but most of the furnishings, paintings, memorials tablets and reredos were lost. The font survived amidst the charred fallen roof timbers, but tragically Chantrey's monument was damaged beyond repair. Restoration of the church was overseen by W.D. Caroe, who designed all the limed-oak furnishings, including the screen in front of the monument, and the new roof. Fragments of Flemish stained glass were salvaged and fitted into the small chancel windows.

The churchyard at Eglwys Newydd has benefited from management with a light hand, and is particularly rich in wildlife. Its gravestones are a record of the social history of the area, with farmers, mineworkers, agents, estate servants and squires of Hafod all to be found there. In 2002-03 the parish carried out various works to improve its paths and safeguard its old trees, and the Hafod Trust restored the cast-iron railings and memorial stone on the Johnes grave.

The Rev. T. Noah Jones in the ruins of the church, with Johnes's Coade stone font – a miraculous survivor of the fire.